Whispers from the First Californians

A Story of California's First People

Front cover:
Antoinette Saubel and
Lenette Saubel, members of the Agua Caliente Band of Cahuilla Indians, dancing at a
Sacramento Gathering.
Photograph by Michele Lasagna, 1975.

Title page:
Thousands of years ago oaks grew in abundance throughout the land of California. This
Valley Oak, one of the oldest oak trees in the San Ramon Valley, in Central California,
yielded hundreds of pounds of acorns for the California Indians. Recently it fell victim to
a new housing tract.
Photograph by Michele Lasagna, 1978.

*Whispers from
the First Californians*

A Story of California's First People

**BY
GAIL FABER and MICHELE LASAGNA
ILLUSTRATIONS BY LOU ANN STYLES and GAIL FABER
MAGPIE PUBLICATIONS • ALAMO, CALIFORNIA**

*Dedicated to the California Indians,
the First People of the Land of California*

ACKNOWLEDGEMENTS

The Authors would like to thank the following people for their particular contributions to this book: Florence Cahill, Nancy DiMaggio, Loretta Head, Vana Parrish Lawson, and Mona Latta Olson. Special thanks to Lou Ann Styles for her art work.

Our deep appreciation to Andrew Andreoli, Hupa, Director of the Indian Teacher Education Personnel Program at Humboldt State University, Arcata, California, for his generous contribution of time and effort in editing this book.

First Edition August 1980   Revised Edition June 1994

Published by Magpie Publications
Post Office Box 636
Alamo, CA. 94507

ISBN: 0-936480-09-2 (student edition-soft cover)
ISBN: 0-936480-10-6 (student edition-hard cover)
ISBN: 0-936480-11-4 (teacher edition)

Dear Reader,

When this textbook, **Whispers From the First Californians**, was first published, there were few textbooks available for students about the California Indians. Since that time, **Whispers From the First Californians** has been read in thousands of classrooms, libraries, and homes throughout California.

Now you are about to read the **new** revised edition of **Whispers From the First Californians**. You will not only learn about the California Indians of long ago, but you will also learn about the California Indians today. As you begin to read you will meet Coyote and Eagle in the Creation Stories. You will read about the tools used every day by Indian women and men. You will read about the Indian women as they gathered seeds, plants, and acorns in the meadows and forests. Perhaps, you will be able to picture an Ohlone Indian stepping into a tule boat and paddling his way through the marshes hunting for bird eggs. You will see the inside of a plank house in Northern California and watch as a brush home is built in the Great Central Valley. You will almost hear the voices of singers with their clapsticks as they accompany Indian dancers dressed in beautiful dance regalia.

As you journey further in the **new Whispers**, you will learn that the California Indians have leaders not chiefs, doctors not medicine men, Gatherings not Pow-Wows, dance regalia not costumes, songs not chants, and stories not legends or myths. In Chapter Twelve you will learn what happened to the Indians when non-Indians arrived in California.

Soon you will know the different names of the California Indians, and be able to locate the areas where they live. Finally, you will meet many of the California Indian people of today—elders, tribal leaders, teachers, singers, dancers, artists, basketweavers, storytellers, school principals and college professors as well as the little girls on the front cover of this book—now grown up.

When you have finished reading **Whispers From the First Californians**, you will have learned many important and wonderful things about the California Indians, and you will understand that the Indians have existed from past to present and are here forever.

The Authors

TABLE OF CONTENTS

CHAPTER FIVE
NATURE'S NOURISHMENT, HUNTING AND FISHING

CHAPTER SIX
USING NATURE'S GIFTS FOR BASKETS, BOWLS, AND BOATS

CHAPTER SEVEN
CLOTHING OF THE INDIANS

CHAPTER EIGHT
HOMES OF THE INDIANS

CHAPTER NINE
CUSTOMS AND CEREMONIES

CHAPTER TEN
MUSIC, ART, AND GAMES

CHAPTER ELEVEN
ISHI, A SPECIAL CALIFORNIAN

CHAPTER TWELVE
CALIFORNIA INDIANS THEN AND NOW

As you read **Whisper**s, you will notice some words are darkened. These words are listed and defined for you in the **glossary** at the back of the book. Small numbers at the end of many sentences and paragraphs refer to the books where the information in that sentence or paragraph was found. These **reference books** are listed after the glossary.

TRIBAL AREAS OF THE CALIFORNIA INDIANS

California Culture Area

Tolowa
Shasta
Modoc
Chilula
Yurok
Karuk
Achumawi
Chimariko
Whilkut
Hupa
Wiyot
Wintu
(Northern)
Atsugewi
Northern Paiute
Mattole
Nongatl
Yana
Sinkyone
Maidu
Lassik
Nomlaki
(Central Wintu)
Wailaki
Konkow
Cahto
Yuki
(Northwest Maidu)
Washoe
Coast Yuki
Patwin
Huchnom
Pomo
(Southern Wintu)
Nisenan
Wappo
(Southern Maidu)
Lake Miwok
Wappo
Mono Lake
Northern Paiute
Coast Miwok
Miwok
Owens Valley
Paiute-Shoshone
Costanoan
(Ohlone)
Northern Valley
Yokuts
Western Shoshone
(Panamint-Koso)
Monache
(Mono)
Esselen
Southern Valley
Yokuts
Tubatulabal
Salinan
Kawaiisu
Southern
Paiute
Kitanemuk
Mojave
Chumash
Tataviam
Serrano
Chemehuevi
Gabrielino
Channel Island Chumash
Cahuilla
Halchidhoma
Juaneno
Luiseno
Cupeno
Tipai
(Diegueno-Kamia-Kumeyaay)
Quechan
(Yuma)
Island Gabrielino
Ipai
(Diegueno)
Baja California
(Mexico)

N

This map shows many of the tribes of the California Indians. The dark line indicates the California Culture Area. The area to the left of the dark line is separated from the Great Basin Culture Area by the Sierra Nevada Mountains. The tribes in the California Culture Area had unique cultures that were different from the other culture areas.

FIRST WHISPERS

Everything was quiet. The chill of the morning air was as yet unbroken by the cry of a bird or animal. Wisps of damp fog drifted through the sleeping foothills and clung to the meadow grass. The treetops along the ridge shone with a soft golden glow as the sun's rays began to bring warmth to nature's world. Bit by bit, sound by sound, nature shed its shadowy blanket of night to welcome the dawning of a California morning.

As the mist cleared, the whispers of nature were joined by the whispers of human voices. Silhouetted against the velvety green slopes of the foothills stood a small group of people—the First Californians. Their eyes followed the flight of a radiant butterfly as it floated over a field of wildflowers. The quiet was undisturbed except for the noisy chatter of magpies searching for berries and seeds in a nearby thicket. A jackrabbit scurried into the shadows, unaccustomed to the sound of human voices. Through this unfolding scene of beauty, nature whispered its welcome to the First Californians.

No one knows when these First People came to California. No one knows just what happened when they did come, but we do know that long, long ago there were no people living in California. There were no people on the whole North American continent! California belonged to the birds, animals, fish, trees, wind, snow, and the rain. It belonged to the grass, wildflowers, rocks, oceans, streams, valleys, mountains, sunsets, clouds, and skies!

XI

Throughout most of California, many Indians honor the Coyote or Eagle as creators of the world. In many creation stories, the Great Spirit/Creator took the form of Coyote or Eagle to create the world. Many tribes believe that Eagle and Coyote were also the creators of the Indian people.

Coyote was a cunning, clever animal and was perhaps more like a person because of his human qualities. Coyote was known for his humor, kindness, generosity, and patience. He was also known to be selfish and boastful and a trickster. Coyote taught the Indians the correct way to live. The Indians respect all animals because the animals are part of the creation stories.

As you read the creation stories in this chapter, you will notice that Coyote is a main character in many of the stories.

CHAPTER ONE
A NEW WORLD

CREATION STORIES OF THE CALIFORNIA INDIANS

Throughout California, Indian people in many different tribes tell **creation stories**. Creation stories tell about the world in the beginning and the creation of the Indian people. These teaching stories have been passed down from **generation to generation** by older people, usually the grandmothers or grandfathers of each tribe. These **elders** tell many things of long ago. They teach the stories that tell the history of their creation. As the elder tells the stories he or she may imitate the actions and voices of the people and animals or birds in the story. Often the elder sings certain parts of the history that he is telling.[1]

There are many creation stories that have been told by tribes throughout California for thousands and thousands of years. As in many **oral histories**, some of the stories may change slightly in the retelling from generation to generation, but the lesson or moral of each story remains the same.[2]

To this very day the people listen carefully to the grandmothers, grandfathers, and elders of their tribe tell the creation stories. These stories will be shared with Indian children of future generations and they, too, will remember how they came to be.

CREATION STORIES FROM NORTHERN CALIFORNIA

The Karuk Indians of Northern California tell this story about the formation of the earth and creation of the people. The story tells how the earth was formed and then how Nagaicho returned to the North after his work on earth was finished.

* THE EARTH DRAGON

"Before this world was formed, it is said, there was another world. The sky of that world was made of Sandstone rock. Two gods, Thunder and Nagaicho, looked at the old sky because it was being shaken by Thunder.

'The Rock is old,' they said. 'We will fix it. We will stretch it out far to the East.'

Then they stretched the Sandstone rock of the sky, walking on the sky as they did so. Under each of the four corners of the sky they set a great rock to hold it. They then made the different things which would make the world pleasant for people to live in. In the South they made flowers, in the East they made a large opening so the clouds could come through, then, in the West they made an opening so the fog from the ocean could come through. To make clouds, they lit the fire. They said the clouds would keep people, who were to be made later, from having headaches because of too much sunshine.

Then, they made Man from Earth. They put grass inside of him to form his stomach. They put the figure to make Man's heart. For his liver they used a round piece of red clay, and the same for his kidneys. For his windpipe they used a reed. Then they prepared blood for Man by red stone, which they pounded into powder and mixed with water.

* The Story "The Earth Dragon," is quoted exactly as it is printed in the Humboldt County Office of Education N.I.C.E. program.

After making the various parts of Man, the two gods took one of his legs, split it and made Woman of it.

Then they made the Sun to travel by day; the Moon to travel by night.

But the creations of the two gods were not to endure because flood waters came. Every day it rained, every night it rained, all the People slept, and then the sky fell. The waters of the oceans came together everywhere. There was no land or mountains or rocks, only water. Trees and grass were not. There were no fish or land animals or birds, as Human Beings and animals alike had been washed away. The wind did not then blow through the portals of the world, nor was there snow, nor frost, nor rain. It did not thunder nor did it lightning. Since there were no trees to be struck, it did not thunder. There was neither clouds, nor fog, nor was there a sun. It was very dark.

Then it was that this earth with its great long horns, got up and walked down this way from the North. As it walked along the deep places, and looked up, the water rose to its shoulders. When it came up into shallower places and looking up, raised the ridge in the North upon which the waves break. He came to the middle of the world, into the East, and to the rising of the Sun, Earth looked up again. There, where it looked up, a large land appeared near to the coast. Far away to the South, Earth continued looking up, and walked under the ground.

Having come from the North and traveled far South, and laid down; the God, Nagaicho, who, standing on Earth's head, had been carried to the South where the Earth now lays down. Placing Earth's head as it should be, Nagaicho spread gray clay between Earth's eyes and on each horn. Upon the clay he placed a layer of reeds, and another layer of clay. And on this he placed grass and brush and trees.

'I have finished,' Nagaicho stated. 'Let there be mountain peaks here on his head. Let the waves of the sea break against them.'

The mountains formed, banks formed on them. The small stones he had placed on Earth's head which was buried from sight, became larger.

At this time People appeared. People all had animal names and later when Indians came to live on this Earth, the First People were changed into animals which still bear their names. Seal, Sea Lion and Grizzly Bear built the Ant's house. One Woman was named Whale. She was fat and that is why there are so many stout Indian women today.

Nagaicho caused different sea food to grow, and also Abalones and Mussels and many other things of the sea grew. He then made Salt from the ocean foam. He made the waters of the ocean rise up in waves and said the ocean should always behave in that way. He said that old Whales would float ashore so People might have them to eat.

He made Redwoods and other trees grow on the tail of the Great Dragon which laid to the North.

He made creeks by dragging his foot through the Earth so People would have good fresh water to drink.

He traveled all over the Earth making things so this Earth would be a comfortable place for Man.

He had a great many Oak trees so People would have plenty of Acorns to eat.

When he had finished making everything, he and his Dog took a walk all over the Earth to see how all the new things looked. Finally, when they arrived at their starting point, he said to his Dog, 'We are close to home, my Dog. Now we should go back North and stay there,' So he left this world, where People live and now lives in the North."

*   *   *   *   *

The following story is from the Achumawi Indians. It was passed on by the elders of the tribe and tells how Coyote created the world and brought fire into the world to keep the Indians from freezing.

* THE STORY OF CREATION

Our earth was created by the coyote and the eagle, or, rather, the coyote began and the eagle completed it. First, the coyote scratched it up with his paws out of nothingness, but the eagle complained that there were no mountains for him to perch on. The coyote made hills, but they were not high enough, so the eagle fell to work on it and scratched up great ridges. When he flew over them his feathers dropped down, took root, and became trees, and his pinfeathers became bushes and plants. But in the creation of animals and man the coyote and the fox participated, the first being an evil spirit, the other good. They quarreled as to whether they should let men live always or not. The coyote said, "If they want to die, let them die"; but the fox said, "If they want to come back, let them come back." But nobody ever came back, for the coyote prevailed. Last of all, the coyote brought fire into the world, for the Indians were freezing. He journeyed far to the west, to a place where there was fire, stole some of it, and brought it home in his ears. He kindled a fire in the mountains, and the Indians saw the smoke of it and went up and got fire so they were warmed and comforted, and have kept it ever since.

* * * * *

* "The Story of Creation" is quoted exactly as it is printed in **Tribes of California** by Stephen Powers, published by the University of California, page 273.

The North Central Indians, such as the Maidu, tell this creation story. It begins with a scene of the world covered with water.

* THE CREATION

In the beginning there was no sun, no moon, no stars. All was dark, and everywhere there was only water. A raft came floating on the water. It came from the North, and in it were two persons—Turtle and Pehe-ipe. The stream flowed very rapidly. Then from the sky a rope of feathers, called Pokelma, was let down, and down it came Earth-Initiate. When he reached the end of the rope, he tied it to the bow of the raft, and stepped in. His face was covered and was never seen, but his body shone like the sun. He sat down, and for a long time said nothing.

At last Turtle said, "Where do you come from?" and Earth-Initiate answered, "I come from above." Then Turtle said, "Brother, can you not make for me some good dry land, so that I may sometimes come up out of the water?" Then he asked another time, "Are there going to be any people in the world?" Earth-Initiate thought awhile, and then said, "Yes". "Turtle asked, "How long before you are going to make people?" Earth-Initiate replied, "I don't know. You want to have some dry land: well, how am I going to get any earth to make it of?" Turtle answered, "If you will tie a rock about my left arm, I'll dive for some," Earth-Initiate did as Turtle asked, and then reaching around, took the end of a rope from somewhere, and tied it to Turtle. When Earth-Initiate came to the raft, there was no rope there: he just reached out and found one. Turtle said, "If the rope is not long enough, I'll jerk it once, and you must haul me up; if it is long enough, I'll give two jerks, and then you must pull me up quickly, as I shall have all the earth that I can carry." Just as Turtle went over the side of the boat, Pehe-ipe began to shout loudly.

---

* The story "The Creation" is quoted exactly as it is printed in **The Way We Lived**, edited with commentary by Malcolm Margolin, published by Heyday Books.

Turtle was gone a long time. He was gone six years; and when he came up, he was covered with green slime, he had been down so long. When he reached the top of the water, the only earth he had was a very little under his nails: the rest had all washed away. Earth-Initiate took with his right hand a stone knife from under his left armpit, and carefully scraped the earth out from under Turtle's nails. He put the earth in the palm of his hand, and rolled it about till it was round; it was as large as a small pebble. He laid it on the stern of the raft. By and by he went to look at it: it had not grown at all. The third time that he went to look at it, it had grown so that it could not be spanned by the arms. The fourth time he looked, it was as big as the world, the raft was aground, and all around were mountains as far as he could see. The raft came ashore at Tadoiko, and the place can be seen today.

* * * * *

CREATION STORIES FROM CENTRAL CALIFORNIA

The Pomo Indians of Central California had many beautiful and interesting stories. The Kashaya band of the Pomo Indian people tell this creation story. Here is a small part of the Kashaya story.

* THE CREATION OF THE OCEAN

This is something from ancient times—I am going to tell about the creation.

Coyote was the smartest of all. He presided just like a heavenly being with his people. And he always used to tell them what to do, as if he were guarding the people. Because he was the smartest of all, he was the leader of his people. Coyote lived with a big group of people.

* The story "The Creation of the Ocean" (told by Herman James, August, 1957) is quoted exactly as it is printed in the book entitled **Kashaya Texts** by Robert L. Oswalt, published by University of California Press, Copyright 1964, pages 37, 39.

At that time there were no human beings; the animal people talked. They spoke a language like the Indian language we are speaking now. That's why they told this story in our fashion, in our language. We still speak the language that they spoke with. Having been given that, they told stories in our language about what Coyote did.

One time he went off into the wilderness. He must have gone a long way. The land was burning hot as he went. There was no water anywhere. Then he found a large opening, a level field. He was sick from thirst. He was really sick from thirst.

He still knew, he had everything in his head, just like Our Father knows; things were easy for him. We tell that he created the world like Our Father did.

Then sitting down, resting on his knees, he looked as far as his eyes could see. Having done so, he picked up a stick, and dug with it. He dug for water although there did not seem to be any anywhere in that dry land. It appeared as if there was no water there where he was.

It was burning hot there where he was sitting. In the old days they set fire to openings there in order to get food—those people had set fire to that opening in order to burn up the grasshoppers, in order to gather the grasshoppers.

Then, suddenly, it looked like there was a little water there where he was digging. He continued digging. Suddenly, water spouted up high, as if it were never to stop. Thereupon he ran away, not because he was afraid, but in order to see from a distance. He ran to the top of a small hill to watch from; there. Then, where that land had been, it was filled completely with water.

Then, at first, he drank some of that water. Afterwards what we call the ocean started to taste salty. The ocean (literally bitter-water) became bitter with what we call ashes. Then he named it after it became a great body of water, saying, "This will be the ocean."

He watched it in the beginning. The water lay still just like a lake with no waves. It looked eerie lying there so still. Then taking a stick, he said, "Do like this!" Making waves, moving the water up and down and making it splash, he said, "Make waves!" Then when he had walked up the hill a little way, the water surged up in high waves; the water was heaving and breaking way over the rocks.

Then he scratched a mark to set the limits to which the water could go—this is the ocean which we see, it rises no further. And after he prepared that, he fixed the limit to the tide. He again scratched a mark to determine how far the tide would go out.

* * * * * *

Andrew Galvan, is a native American Indian consultant and member of the Ohlone tribe. He tells this creation story that he learned from his father, who, in turn learned the story from his mother, who had heard the story from her grandfather.

* HOW GRANDFATHER CREATED THE WORLD

Long, long ago Grandfather was out in the Universe where he lives. He saw a great blue ball of water. He wanted to go visit it, but it was a very long journey to go from the place where Grandfather lived to this place we call Earth. Grandfather decided he would become an Eagle and fly off to visit the Earth. Grandfather, in the form of an Eagle, began the long journey. He began flying through the skies. Suddenly, Grandfather came into the middle of a group of meteors. He was knocked down. So Grandfather flew home. Grandfather still wanted to go and see the place the people called Earth. So Grandfather plucked a feather from his wing and put his whole spirit into the feather.

He said, "I'll send this feather on a long journey and I'll put my spirit in this feather. That way I can go visit the place they call Earth."

The feather was sent on the long journey to earth. At that time the Earth was all water. The feather landed in the water and started a spinning whirlpool. Grandfather, in the spirit of the feather, had started the whirlpool and then Grandfather's spirit started to draw the world with the feather. He drew the hills, mountains, valleys, plants, oceans, rivers, creeks, and streams. Grandfather also drew people. He drew each person with a different face. Today, if you look at all the faces, you will see that each one is different.

* * * * *

* This story is quoted from the oral stories told by Andrew Galvan in November, 1992.

The earliest known written version of an Indian account about Mount Diablo appeared in an 1859 San Francisco publication Hesperian Magazine. Since the story tells of the San Francisco Bay Area, it may be a Miwok or Ohlone story. In this account Coyote and Eagle decide to create earth from a world covered by water. Two mountain peaks rise from the waters. One peak is Mount Diablo and across the water is Mount Reed.

* TRADITION OF THE CALIFORNIA INDIANS

There was once a time when there were no human inhabitants in California, but there were two spirits, one evil, the other good. They made war one upon another, and the good one overcome the evil. At that time the entire face of the country was covered with water, except two islands, one of which was Mount Diablo, the other Reed's Peak. There was a coyote on the peak, the only living thing there. One day the coyote saw a feather floating on the water, and, as it reached the island, suddenly turned into an eagle, and spreading its broad pinions, flew upon the mountain. Coyote was much pleased with his new companion, and they lived in great harmony together, making occasional excursions to the other island, coyote swimming while the eagle flew. After some length of time they counseled together and concluded to make Indians; they did so, and as the Indians increased the waters decreased, until where the lake had been became dry land. At that time what is now known as the Golden Gate was an entire chain of mountains, so that you could go from one side to the other dryshod. There were at this time two outlets for the waters, one was Russian River, and other San Juan, at the Parkado. Some time afterwards a great earthquake severed the chain of mountains, and formed what is now known as the Golden Gate. Then the waters of the Great Ocean and the Bay were permitted to mingle. The rocky wall being rent asunder, it was not long before the "pale faces"

* The story, "Tradition of the California Indians," is quoted as printed in **Hesperian Magazine**, Volume 3, page 326, 1859.

found their way in, and as the waters decreased at the coming of the Indians, so have the Indians decreased at the approach of the white man, until the warwhoop is heard no more, and the council fire is no more lighted; for the Indians, like shadows, have passed silently away from the land of the coyote and the eagle.

* * * * *

The stories that follow are from the Salinan Indians of South Central California. They tell of the beginning of the world and the creation of men and women. The stories are very long and only parts are included here.

* THE BEGINNING OF THE WORLD

"After the deluge the eagle wished to get some earth. First, duck dove into the water but failed to bring up any earth. Then the eagle put a heavy weight on the back of the kingfisher and he dove into the water for the earth and succeeded in reaching the bottom. The sea was so deep that when he came to the surface, he was dead. Between his claws the eagle found some earth and after reviving the kingfisher he took the dirt and made the world. Then he revived all the other animals who had been drowned in the deluge, the coyote next after the kingfisher. When the coyote found himself alive again, he shouted out for joy and ran around reviving the rest of the animals that he found dead, sending them back to the eagle."

* * * * *

* The story "The Beginning of the World," (Collected by Dr. H. W. Henshaw, 1884), is quoted exactly as it is printed in the book entitled **The Salinan Indians of California** by Betty Brusa, published by Naturegraph Publishers, Inc.

* THE CREATION OF MEN AND WOMEN

"When the world was completed, there was as yet no people, but the eagle was the chief of the animals. He saw that the world was incomplete and decided to make some people. From some of the earth brought up by the kingfisher he modeled the figure of a man and laid him on the ground. In the beginning he was very small but grew rapidly until he reached normal size. But as yet, he had no life; he was still asleep. Then the eagle stood and admired his work. 'It is impossible,' said he, 'that he should be left alone; he must have a mate.' So he pulled out a feather and laid it beside the sleeping man. Then he left them and went off a short distance, for he knew that a woman was being formed from the feather. But the man was still asleep and did not know what was happening. When the eagle decided that the woman was about completed, he returned, awoke the man by flapping his wings over him and flew away.

The man opened his eyes and stared at the woman. 'What does this mean?' he asked. 'I thought I was alone!' Then the eagle returned and said with a smile, 'I see you have a mate!' Then he sent the newly-made couple out into the world."

* * * * *

* The story, "The Creation of Men and Women," (Collected by Dr. H. W. Henshaw, 1884), is quoted exactly as it is printed in the book entitled **The Salinan Indians of California** by Betty Brusa, published by Naturegraph Publishers, Inc.

CREATION STORIES FROM SOUTHERN CALIFORNIA

In Southern California certain bands of the Chumash people, tell this story about the making of man. Many years ago this story was told to Mr. J.P. Harrington, a man who was very interested in the California Indians.

* THE MAKING OF MAN

After the flood Snilemun (the Coyote of the Sky), Sun, Moon, Morning Star, and Slo?w (the great eagle that knows what is to be) were discussing how they were going to make man, and Slo?w and Snilemun kept arguing about whether or not the new people should have hands like Snilemun. Coyote announced that there would be people in this world and they should all be in his image since he had the finest hands. Lizard was there also, but he just listened night after night and said nothing. At last Snilemun won the argument, and it was agreed that people were to have hands just like his. The next day they all gathered around a beautiful table-like rock that was there in the sky, a very fine white rock that was perfectly symmetrical and flat on top, and of such fine texture that whatever touched it left an exact impression. Snilemun was just about to stamp his hand down on the rock when Lizard, who had been standing silently just behind, quickly reached out and pressed a perfect hand-print into the rock himself. Snilemun was enraged and wanted to kill Lizard, but Lizard ran down into a deep crevice and so escaped. And Slo?w and Sun approved of Lizard's actions, so what could Snilemun do? They say that the mark is still impressed on the rock in the sky. If Lizard had not done what he did, we might have hands like a coyote today.

* * * * *

* The story, "The Making of Man," is quoted exactly as it is printed in **December's Child, A Book of Chumash Oral Narratives**, collected by J. P. Harrington, edited by Thomas Blackburn, published by University of California Press, 1975, page 95.

The Cahuilla Indians of Southern California tell this creation story. It tells the story of the first people and how UMNAW, the Creator of the land, the earth, the water, the air, watches his people, their lives, their living, their food, their homes.

* THE CREATION

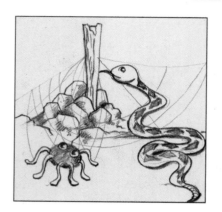

"In the beginning there was nothing but nights, and other Indian words call them the two nights—man and woman...They tried to produce a child, but the child was lost before time for its birth. For four times the same happened and then with a flash of lightning came strong twin boys.

The name of the first one was Mo-Cot and the name of the second was Tem-Ma-Ya-Wit, meaning Creator. These were the first people. They were sitting in the air. There was no earth, no water, no light, nothing but darkness; so they could not see each other, but they could hear each other. They did not call each other 'brother,' but 'my man.'

Now this Mo-Cot, he asked, 'What are we going to do, my man?'

Tem-Ma-Ya-Wit answered, 'You should know, my man.'

Mo-Cot said, 'We must create now.'

Then Mo-Cot created first tobacco. And Tem-Ma-Ya-Wit invented the pipe and gave it two names; Man and Woman...

...Together they made a *who ya no hut*. This is like a bishop's staff, which is carried in the church today. This they tried to stand up, but it could not stand, because there was nothing for it to stand on. So they put a *tem em la wit* (bedrock) to steady the *who ya no hut*, and yet it would not be steady, for it was growing up all of the time.

Now this was the first beginning of the earth. It was the foundation stone, and is in the middle of the world today. Then they created two kinds of snakes to hold it, but they could not hold it.

* The story, "The Creation," is quoted exactly as it is printed in the book entitled **Stories and Legends of the Palm Springs Indians** by Chief Francisco Patencio, published by Palm Springs Desert Museum.

They made a big pile of stones and put them around the *who ya no hut*, and yet it was not steady so they created great spiders, black ones and white ones (not the spiders of today, but the ones that live in the ends of the world), to weave threads to help hold it steady...

...So then they made *pal no cit*, the water ocean. Then they turned up the edges of the earth, so the water could not run over, and the earth became steady, as we see it today.

Tem-Ma-Ya-Wit asked Mo-Cot, 'How are we going to make *no cot em* (people) like ourselves?'

Mo-Cot answered, 'We have made the earth, two kinds: *fam av si*l (meaning moist earth) and *pal lis ma wit* (meaning damp earth). Also the *u le wit* (meaning the clay earth), the *ta vi wit* (meaning the white clay and also the black clay, the yellow clay and the red clay). Of this earth which we have made will we make the people.'

...Then Mo-Cot and Tem-Ma-Ya-Wit saw all the people that they had made, and they called them *No cot em* and *Ta ba tem*, which mean, 'those that have been created.'

...Now, after everything had settled and become quiet again, the people could see well, and they saw that they were of different color. For the white clay had made white people, and black clay had made black people, and yellow clay had made the yellow people, and the red clay had made red people, and each color of people went together.

Then it was that the white-clay people were not pleased about being the only ones without color. They cried to be dark, like the rest. They put different clay on themselves, but it was not good. It came right off after a while.

Then the people called to Mo-Cot that the people were going away. The white people went first, and Mo-Cot said, 'Let them go. They are different. They will always be different.'

Then Mo-Cot saw in the daylight that the colored people were fast going from him. He reached quickly behind him and grasped the *red* people. These were the people that he kept with him. His creation children left him and so it has been to this day, that the children go on away, instead of staying with the parents. As things were done in the first beginning, so they have done ever since."

* * * * *

Andrew Galvan is a descendant of the Ohlone Indian tribe native to the San Francisco Bay Area. His ancestors, who were taken into the mission system by the Franciscan padres, built seven of the Bay Area missions.

Andrew lives in Mission San Jose, California. He has graduated from Hayward State University with a degree in history. He is currently continuing his studies in history.

Andrew is also a Native American Indian Consultant and speaks to many groups of young people about his Ohlone Indian culture and traditions. He is involved in efforts to see that information about America's ancient past is preserved for the benefit of future generations. He believes that the Ohlone people need to know more about their ancestors. By learning about their past, Ohlone children of today and the children of generations to come, can appreciate the achievements of Native American culture.

Storytelling has always been an important tradition of the California Indians. The Storytellers in this photo are (from left) Julian Lang and Nancy Richardson, members of the Karuk tribe and Loren Bommelyn, a member of the Tolowa tribe. These people tell stories that teach about the creation of the Indian people and the history of their tribes. The stories of the past teach lessons that can still be used today. Storytelling keeps traditions of the California Indians alive and connects the past to the present.

You have just read several creation stories of some California Indian tribes. The Indians know that these creation stories tell of the beginning of their lives in this world. Scientists, however, tell another story about the way the first men and women came to the North American **continent**. A scientific story is called a **theory**. A theory is something that is being explored and may not as yet be a proven fact.

A SCIENTIFIC THEORY

Scientists say that 8,000 to 12,000 years ago people walked from[3] one continent to another on a **vast** land/ice bridge joining Asia and Alaska. According to scientists, this land/ice bridge, now known as the **Bering Strait**, extended from North of Wrangell Island and as far south as the Aleutian Islands—a distance of 1,300 miles!

Scientists say that people were able to cross the land/ice bridge because water did not cover this route. The scientific story tells that people searching for food followed the tracks of animals such as the wooly mammoth, the sloth, and the saber-tooth tiger across this land/ice bridge.

As the ice melted, the changing water level slowly began to rise and cover this 1,300 mile wide area. Scientists believe that the people who had crossed from Asia to Alaska stayed in North America.[4]

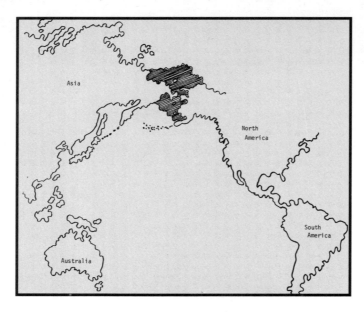

Some scientific theories say that the first people came to the North American continent across a land/ice bridge joining Asia and Alaska.

In 1929, Mr. Malcolm Rogers, an archeologist from the San Diego Museum of Man excavated a site near the ocean in Del Mar, California. Mr. Malcolm Rogers found the skeletal remains of a person referred to as Del Mar Man.

There have been may arguments concerning the age of the skeletal remains of Del Mar Man. Some scientists have dated the remains at 48,000 years old. Other scientists give a date of only 15,000 years old.

Scientists know that Del Mar Man, an ancient Californian, was between age 20 and age 40 at the time of his death. His skull was long and large with a sloping forehead. His lower jaw was large with a pointed chin. His height is not known. An artist named Mary Butler drew this picture of what she believed Del Mar Man, an ancient Californian, looked like 15,000 to 48,000 years ago.

ARCHEOLOGICAL SITES

There are many **archeological sites** that scientists have **excavated**. Archeological sites are places where evidence of human life has been found. These archeological sites prove that Indians have been in the Americas for thousands and thousands of years.

In 1977-1978, during an excavation, archeologists from Riverside near Los Angeles, California, came upon some of the oldest footprints ever found in North America. These footprints were made by a family of Indians as they walked along the banks of the Mojave River in San Bernardino County. The footprints date back more then 6,000 years.[5]

In 1929, Mr. Malcolm Rogers, an archeologist from the San Diego Museum of Man, made an important find. As he excavated a site near the San Dieguito River in Del Mar, California, he came upon skeletal remains of a person referred to as Del Mar Man. At that time there were few ways of dating ancient remains, but today, there are several ways of dating archeological finds. These ways include **radiocarbon**, **geological**, and **geomorphological dating** methods.[6] The discovery in 1929 made by Mr. Rogers was dated at 48,000 years old. Archeologists, however, will not accept this date until dating methods are more accurate. Today's modern methods of dating can only date ancient remains to about 12,000 or 15,000 thousand years ago, but the Indian people know that their beginnings go back to the creation of time.

INTERESTING THOUGHTS

The creation stories of the California Indians tell the stories of how the Indians came to be. The Indians know that their beginnings lie in the earth of the California valleys, mountains, and rivers. The Indians were the first people to hear the whisperings of nature as they walked among the wildflowers and reeds of the hills and valleys. They saw the tule fog drift over the mighty oaks and grassy fields. They watched as the first rays of sunlight turned the blanket of night into a new day. From the beginning, the Indians have been part of the first whispers of California. How marvelous it must be to have a heritage that reaches back in time and touches the dawning of a new world!

BACKTRACKING

Can you answer the following questions?
(1) Why do Indians tell creation stories?

(2) As the stories were told from generation to generation, do you think any of these stories may have changed? Why or why not?

(3) Which California Indian creation story did you like the best? Why?

(4) According to scientific theory about the Bering Strait, why did the first people cross the land/ice bridge from Asia and come to the North American continent?

(5) What types of animals were alive at the time of the land/ice bridge?

(6) Look up radiocarbon dating in an encyclopedia. Tell how this method determines the age of once living material.

Andrew Galvan speaks to many groups of young people about his Ohlone culture and traditions.

Nancy Richardson is a member of the Karuk Indian tribe of Northern California. She is a teacher, basketmaker, singer, and storyteller. Nancy is the Language Program Director at Humboldt State University in Arcata, California. Nancy is a member of a committee for the Advocates for Indigenous California Language Survival and has worked to preserve Indian languages for more than 21 years. Nancy also works closely with Karuk, Yurok, Tolowa, and Hupa language teachers. She is a member of the Karuk Language Restoration Committee, a group that was founded to bring back the disappearing Karuk language.

The languages of many California Indian groups are starting to disappear. There are many different ways the California Indians feel the loss of their language. Many people have not heard the language spoken by anyone at all for years. When a person's language is not spoken, a person may feel sad. Sometimes there is a loss of some part of the family history and culture when a person does not know his or her native language.

Today Indians from the Tolowa, Hupa, Karuk, Ohlone, Luiseno, Cahuilla, Pomo and other tribes go into local schools to teach the languages of their people. Some Indians who have learned to speak their native language, teach the language to their children. Summer camps for Indian children also give hope for the survival of California Indian languages. With helpful people like Nancy Richardson, working with languages in many different ways, native California languages will survive.*

*Hinton, Leanne. "Keeping the Languages Alive" in **News from Native California**. Volume 6, Number 4. Berkeley, California: Heyday Books, Fall 1992, pp. 25-31.

CHAPTER TWO
CALIFORNIA'S FIRST INHABITANTS

The first people in California were the Indians. In the early times before the Spanish came, there were about 310,000 Indians living in California.[1]

Throughout California there were many different Indian languages spoken with many, many more **dialects**. A dialect is a pattern or different form of speech that comes from the main language. Altogether, the California Indians spoke more than 64 languages and an enormous number of dialects.[2] Those who spoke the same language sometimes lived together in the same tribe or group.

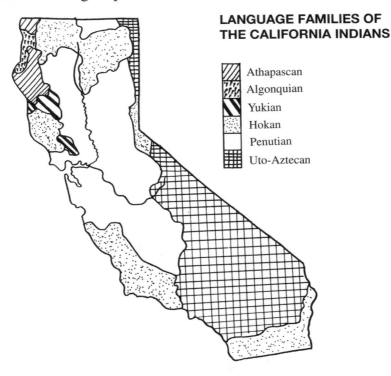

LANGUAGE FAMILIES OF THE CALIFORNIA INDIANS

- Athapascan
- Algonquian
- Yukian
- Hokan
- Penutian
- Uto-Aztecan

As shown on this map, there are six large Indian language families in California. There could be as few as one tribe or as many as one hundred tribes living in the area of each large language family. Each tribe within the large language family spoke a different tribal language often with many dialects. Although the tribal languages and dialects were very different from each other, they all came from the larger language family.

The Indians lived in all areas of California. They lived along the sea-coast and in the mountains, valleys, and deserts. Usually a tribe's name meant "The People." Sometimes the people of one tribe, called the members of another tribe by the name of the location where they lived.[3]

There were differences among the food, clothing, and homes of the California Indians due to the **life zones** of California. When we talk about life zones, we mean the earth's areas where certain animals, climate and plant life exist such as rivers, valleys, mountains, coast lands, and deserts. Due to these differences in life zones, each California Indian tribe lived in different ways. For example, the tribes living along the seacoast such as the Yurok, Wiyot, Coast Miwok, and Chumash ate shellfish, squid, sea bass, and other foods from the sea. The Great Central Valley Indians such as the Yokuts had tule elk, deer, ducks, geese, and jack rabbits as part of their diet. The Indians living in the desert such as the Mojave, Yuma, and Cahuilla used cactus fruits and **mesquite** in their daily meals. Although Indians in different life zones of California ate different foods, one food was common-ly used by most of the tribes in California. Indians gathered or traded for this staple food—acorns.

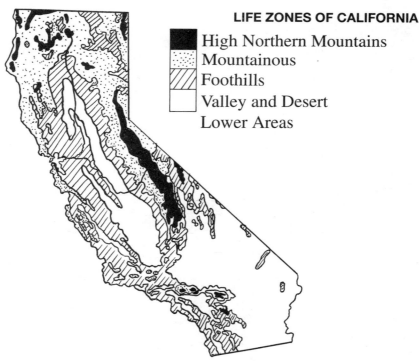

LIFE ZONES OF CALIFORNIA
High Northern Mountains
Mountainous
Foothills
Valley and Desert
Lower Areas

Some California Indians lived on tribal lands that covered several different life zones. Life zones are the earth's areas where certain animals, climate, and plant life exist such as val-leys, mountains, coast lands, and deserts.

WOMEN'S BELONGINGS AND TOOLS

When the California Indians journeyed to collect acorns, attend special ceremonies, or move to temporary camps, they always traveled on foot. The women carried most of the family belongings.[4] Some family belongings included digging sticks, rabbit skin blankets, stirring paddles, looped sticks, and baskets for cooking.[5] Indian women also carried personal belongings. Personal belongings might include **teasel** brushes, shell necklaces, basket caps, bone needles, **obsidian** or **chert** blades for scraping, game sticks, and a small **mortar** and **pestle** for pounding seeds. The Indian women did not carry their belongings everywhere they went. Their belongings stayed at their home camp until the Indians needed to move. Different items were carried on journeys depending on the purpose of the journey.

Most of the Indian women used large **burden** baskets to carry their belongings. A burden basket was supported on a woman's back by a **tump line** or head strap that fit over the woman's forehead and hung down her back and around or under the basket. The tump line was made of **Indian hemp**, **milkweed fiber**, **nettle**, wild iris leaves,[6] or other natural fibers and was long and wide like a strap. The tump line made it possible for women and sometimes men to carry extremely heavy loads.[7]

The woman on the left is carrying some of her belongings in a net. Basket caps were sometimes used to prevent chafing or irritations of the skin. The woman on the right is using a headband made of plant fiber to support a burden basket on her back.

Some Indian women wore basket caps to help ease their loads. A tump line fit over the basket cap. The cap helped protect the person's forehead from becoming scratched or irritated by the tump line and the weight of the filled basket. The Karuk, Hupa, Yurok, Achumawi, Modoc, Maidu, and Cahuilla women represented some of the tribes who wore basket caps when carrying burden baskets. Other women such as the Yokuts used only the tump line with no cap to support their burden baskets.[8]

In some tribes such as the Karuk, basket caps were used by both men and women. The Karuk men wore basket caps to help steady twelve foot dip-net-poles on their heads when salmon fishing.

Many Indian women used bag-like nets to carry their belongings. The nets were made of milkweed, nettle, hemp, or **agave** fibers. The nets looked like small hammocks, gathered at the ends on heavy loops. The loops were joined by heavy cords that fit over the forehead. The bag-like net was used by the women of the Yokuts and Koso tribes as well as many other Southern California tribes.

Another type of net used by the Yuki and also the Pomo tribes was a net with the ends woven into a long headband that fit over the wearer's forehead. The net hung down the wearer's back.[9]

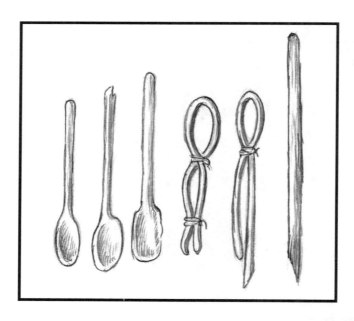

These are Indian women's belongings and work tools. The first three tools are wooden paddles used for stirring boiling mush in a cooking basket. The next two tools are looped sticks for lifting hot rocks from the fire and for putting the rocks into the water or mush. The digging stick was used for digging roots and loosening dirt.

MEN'S BELONGINGS AND TOOLS

Indian men had many different tools and belongings. Among these were bows and arrows, deer antlers and stone **wedges** for splitting wood, bone **awls** for sewing rabbit skin blankets or animal skin capes, and a flat piece of wood for starting a fire. Several sharp pointed deer antlers for chipping chert, obsidian, or **jasper** into **arrowheads** were also part of a man's belongings.

Men used many types of fishing tools such as long spears for jabbing fish and nets made of fine roots or grasses. They also used basket traps for eel. Hooks made of shell or bone and sinkers made of stone were also fishing tools. Often **charmstones** were carved from **steatite** or other stones. These charmstones were hung near a pond or river to bring more fish into the area. Charms for good luck in hunting were sometimes worn around the neck.[10]

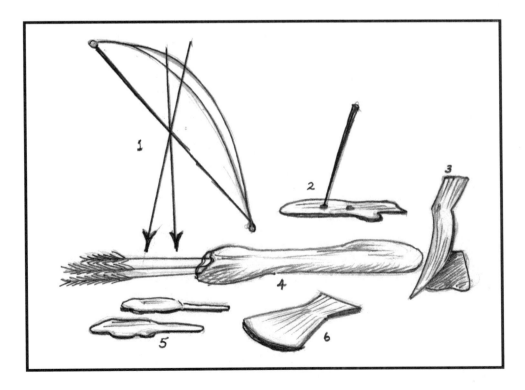

These are Indian men's belongings. Included are (1) bow and arrows (2) wood and drilling stick for starting a fire (3) elk antler wedge (4) quiver and arrows (5) awls (6) stone wedge for splitting logs.

Another tool commonly used by men of the Karuk, Yurok, and Hupa tribes was an **adze**. An adze is made from stone or bone and shell and is used for scraping and chopping. With an adze an Indian could shape a log and hollow it out. Most wood is too hard for this tool so the Indians burned the wood first. The partly burned wood was easier to scrape with this tool. The adze was used mostly by the Yuroks of Northern California for making dug-out canoes.[11]

Arrow straighteners were carried by many California Indians. The Yokuts used an arrow straightener made of steatite that could be heated in a fire. A groove the size of an **arrowshaft** was chipped into the steatite. When the steatite was heated, the arrowshaft was moved back and forth in the heated groove. This would straighten out a bent or crooked arrowshaft.

Another kind of arrow straightener was also used. A crooked arrowshaft was pulled through a hole in a heated flat piece of steatite. Water sprinkled on the wooden arrowshaft caused the wood to steam and the crooked part of the shaft straightened as it cooled.

A third type of straightener was made of wood with a hole in it. The arrowshaft was pulled through the hole. The wood straightener was used by the Indians of Northern California.[12]

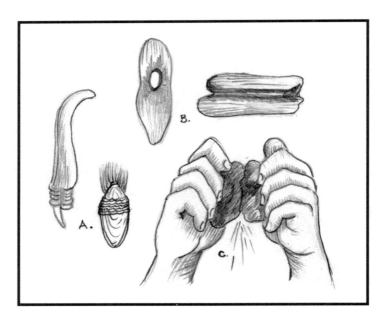

A. This is the front and side view of an adze. A piece of mussel shell was tightly tied to a curved bone. The bone was used as a handle and the shell used for scraping.
B. These are arrow straighteners made of stone.
C. Some Indians struck two pieces of quartz or flint together to make sparks and start a fire.

BOWS AND ARROWS

One of the most important tools used by the Indian men was the bow and arrow. Indian men took special care of their bows and arrows.

Bows were made from sturdy pieces of wood such as cedar or yew. Bows were often polished with deer bone **marrow** to keep them in good condition. Sometimes one man in a tribe was especially good at making bows. He would make bows for other members of his tribe and was often such an expert craftsman that Indians from neighboring tribes traded treasured items for these special bows.

There were many different types of arrowshafts, but most Indians used two-piece arrowshafts. The main shaft of the arrow was sometimes made of hollow cane and a shorter piece of wood or **foreshaft** could fit into the hollow end of the cane. An arrowhead was attached to the end. The Indians who used a foreshafted arrow found it valuable because when the arrow was shot into an animal, only the main shaft need be removed and another foreshaft attached in order for the hunter to shoot again. If an arrow was ruined, the hunter only lost the foreshaft of the arrow and not the entire shaft.[13]

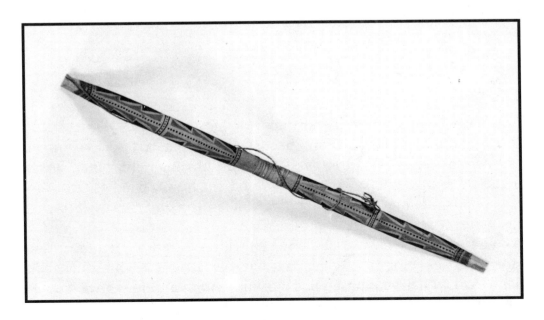

Hupa Bow

California Indians knew how to chip obsidian, chert, and other hard stones into arrowheads. Men put these pointed arrowheads on the ends of wooden shafts to make arrows or spears. Some of these arrowheads were large and others smaller depending on the type of animals the men were hunting. Indian men spent many long hours chipping arrowheads. They also used obsidian or chert to make tools to remove skins from animals they had killed.

This collection of stone tools includes Pomo arrowheads and obsidian blades and cutting tools used by the Indians who lived along the Klamath River in Northern California.

INTERESTING THOUGHTS

You have been reading about many of the belongings and tools of the California Indians. The Indians used California's **natural resources** to make their belongings and tools. They used obsidian and other stones for arrowheads and scrapers. They used wood for bows, paddles, and digging sticks. Shells, steatite, and antlers were used for other tools. Fibers from plants were woven into nets and tump lines.

As you read on, you will see how the Indians used the natural resources for food, homes, clothing, boats, and baskets. It was a bountiful land. The Indians worked hard gathering and storing food, building homes, and caring for the needs of their families. They treated the land with respect and gave thanks to the Great Spirit for the many gifts that had been given to them.

BACKTRACKING

Can you answer the following questions?

(1) Where did the Indians settle in California? Why did they choose these areas?

(2) List several belongings for Indian men and women and tell why each was important.

(3) What is obsidian? How was it used by the Indians?

(4) What are natural resources? Why were they important to the Indians?

An important tool for every Indian man was a fire drill. Indians had no matches to start a fire. They used a flat piece of wood with a few holes on one side. The Indians of Northwestern California used cottonwood roots. The holes in the wood were not deep. The Indians twirled a pointed stick on one of the holes until the wood got hotter and hotter. They laid some fine, dry leaves near the hole, and when the wood was very hot, this tinder began to burn. Tinder is very dry and easily catches fire. With the burning tinder they started a larger fire.

Alice Frank, Yurok, is wearing a necklace made of dentalium shells. Dentalium shells were used as a form of trade money by the tribes of Northwestern California. This photo was taken in 1907.

CHAPTER THREE
TRADE AMONG THE INDIANS

When the Indians journeyed, the main purpose was to gather foods, such as acorns, seeds, roots, seaweed, mesquite, and agave. Another important reason for a journey was to trade with other tribes. In most tribes, individuals or groups traveled to other tribes to trade certain goods. Important men in some tribes had special trading partners in other tribes. Often these people were relatives.[1]

Trading between tribes took place on friendly visits or at **Gatherings** and **Big Times** when there was a surplus of foods or goods to be traded.[2] Trading was important to all Indians because through trading, they could obtain food items that might be in short supply, such as acorns. The Indians also traded for goods that were not available in the area where they lived. For example, some areas of California lacked certain resources, such as good wood for bows, obsidian for arrowheads, certain materials for basket making, salt, **cinnabar** for red coloring, shells or steatite for bowls, charms, tools, and carvings. Trading among the tribes was valuable because it allowed the Indians to gain goods that otherwise they may not have had.

Indians in Northern California such as the Hupa, traded with their neighbors, the Yuroks, who lived on the coast. The Hupa Indians often traded seeds, nuts, and deerskins for redwood canoes, dried fish, seaweed, and bow wood. A Hupa Indian might have traded a bow, a fur quiver, and many arrows for a good boat. The Yuroks may have exchanged a boat, deerskins, red woodpecker skins, or tools for bows and arrows.[3]

Yurok redwood canoes were highly prized as trade items among the Indians of Northern California. Today, there are a few Yurok boat builders who continue to use ancient techniques to build beautiful redwood canoes.

TRIBAL AREAS OF THE CALIFORNIA INDIANS

This map shows many of the tribes of the California Indians. The dark line indicates the California Culture Area. The area to the left of the dark line is separated from the Great Basin Culture Area by the Sierra Nevada Mountains. The tribes in the California Culture Area had unique cultures that were different from the other culture areas.

The Yuki people in Northern California traded with their neighbors, the Nomlaki. The Yuki traded deerskins, pinenuts, and seeds for salt and dried fish from the Nomlaki.[4]

The Indians of the Sacramento Delta Area traded with their neighbors for wooden fishhooks, bird bone whistles, and bird figures of baked clay.[5]

Near Drake's Bay in Marin County, **basalt** mortars, some weighing from 20 to 125 pounds were found. Archeologists believe that these mortars were traded and carried to Drake's Bay from as far away as 25 miles.[6]

Indians in Southern California, such as the Gabrielino, traded with the Coastal Island Indians for steatite. This soft stone was traded either in a rough form or chipped, carved, and shaped into bowls. These bowls were traded to many groups such as the Chumash, Yokuts, Ipai, Tipai, Luiseno, Serrano, and by the Chumash to the distant Tubatulabal.[7] The Gabrielino Indians also traded steatite, shells, dried fish, sea otter pelts, and salt with the Serranos. In exchange, the Serranos gave the Gabrielinos acorns, seeds, obsidian, and deerskins.[8]

Throughout California the food items most traded by the Indians were salt, acorns, fish, pinenuts, dried shellfish meat, seaweed, kelp, seeds, nuts, animal meat, and berries. The most important non-food trade items and also the oldest trade items were marine shells and beads made from these shells. Other important non-food trade items were obsidian, baskets, hides and fur pelts, and bows.[9]

Tribes not only traded with other tribes, but they also traded within their own groups. At times, the Pomo, the Nomlaki, and the Chumash traded among their own people. For example, the Chumash group was such a large tribe that the Chumash people living along the coast would trade with the Island Chumash living on the islands off the coast. Beads, steatite, shells, and otter skins from the Island Chumash were traded to the Coast Chumash for acorns, pinenuts, **chia** seeds, rabbit and deerskins, wild cherries, baskets, and **serpentine** bowls. The Coast Chumash also traded with the Inland Chumash living in the valleys east of them. The Inland Chumash would come to the coast to trade for shellfish, starfish, baskets, steatite, and arrowheads.[10]

TRADE MONEY

The California Indians used several different kinds of materials as trade money. The most common materials used were clamshells, **dentalium** shells, and stones called magnesite. Dentalium shells and strings of beads made from clamshells were used over large areas of California for trading, decorations, gifts, or as personal items to show wealth.[11]

CLAMSHELL BEADS

Several different kinds of shells were used by the Indians of California as trade money. Clamshell **disk** beads were the most common type of shell bead used over most of California.[12] The beads were traded from tribe to tribe and have been found as far away as Arizona.[13] Some tribes such as the Maidu, often traded for broken pieces of clamshells. They rounded and smoothed their own beads from these pieces.[14]

Clamshell beads were among the hardest and longest lasting form of shell beads in California.[15] Large clams were found and collected in Bodega Bay north of San Francisco by the Coast Miwok and their neighbors, the Pomo Indians. The Pomo Indians became the main suppliers of clamshell beads for all of Central California.[16] Another type of large clam was collected by the Chumash Indians in Morro Bay near San Luis Obispo. These clams were collected as far south as San Diego. The Chumash Indians supplied most of the clamshell beads for Southern California.[17]

Clam shells and clamshell beads were traded by the Pomo, Chumash, and other Indians living along the coast to almost all the tribes in California. The shells were broken into pieces and each piece was ground on a rough stone until it was a smooth, round disk. A **hand pump drill** was used to make holes in the center of each disk. The shells were strung on string and then rolled and smoothed by hand on a slab of rock. Drilling holes and smoothing the disks took many hours of patient work. The value of each bead depended on the size, the thickness, and the polish or color of the disk. Older strings of beads were highly prized because the more the beads were handled, the glossier and more polished the beads became.[18] Many Indians often kept these beads and wore them as a sign of wealth. The beads were passed down from generation to generation.[19] Today, many California Indians continue the tradition of making clamshell disk beads.

Clamshells were used over large areas of California for trading, decorations, gifts, or as personal items to show wealth. In the picture, Captain Tom's wife, a Southern Maidu or Nisenan, is wearing a 10-yard necklace of 1,160 money beads made of clamshells and a deerskin belt and headband decorated with abalone. The photograph was taken in 1874.

DENTALIUM SHELLS

Dentalium shells were used as a form of trade money by the tribes of Northwestern California. These included the Tolowa, Hupa, Karuk, Wintu, Yurok, and other tribes as far south as the Pomo. Dentalium shells came from the north near Vancouver Island.[20] These shells were shaped like small tusks or teeth. They were more highly valued by the Northwestern Indians than other common shells such as **haliotis** (abalone), **olivella**, and clamshells.[21]

The Northwestern Indians used only the dentalium shells that were 1⅞ inches or longer for trade money. Some Indian traders had **tattoos** on their arm so they could measure each shell. The most valuable shell was 2½ inches long.[22] The people decorated these shells with fishskin, or snakeskin and tipped them with the down of a red woodpecker.[23] Dentalium shells or strings of dentalium shells were wrapped in soft fur such as mink or rabbit or carried in a hand-carved elkhorn case.[24] The strings of the largest dentalium shells were considered so valuable that they were kept as wealth items.[25]

The elk horn purse was used by the Northwest Indians of California to carry dentalium.

MAGNESITE

The Pomo Indians who lived near Clear Lake found a stone called magnesite.[26] This stone was not very hard and could be ground into small tube-like pieces 1 to 3 inches in length. The stone was heated in a fire, cooled and polished. During this preparation, the magnesite turned shades of pink, red, or gold. The Pomo Indians strung the magnesite beads with clamshell beads. The magnesite beads were highly prized for trading and often more valuable then dentalium shells. Magnesite was too valuable to be sold or traded by the string. Magnesite beads were traded individually or placed in the middle of lengths of clamshell beads.[27]

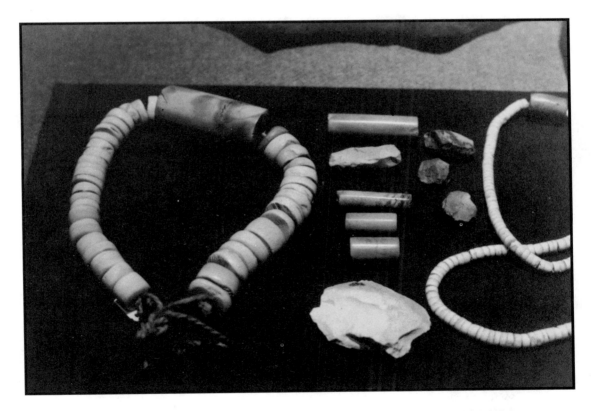

When magnesite is heated and polished, it turns shades of pink, red or gold. When magnesite is strung with clamshell beads, it is a very beautiful neck piece.

TRADE ROUTES

The trade routes that the Indians used went north and south as well as east and west. These routes had been used for thousands and thousands of years. Some routes went from one village to the next village or if the trail crossed the desert, the routes might go from one water spring to the next. On the longer routes, the traders usually traveled only short distances, but the goods they carried could be traded again and again and be passed on for hundreds of miles from where the goods had started. One trade route went along the coast between the mountains and stretched from the San Francisco Bay Area to the San Diego Bay Area. There was another trade route that followed the San Joaquin River through the Great Central Valley and across the lands of the Yokuts.

Indians from Nevada and Arizona tribes used their own desert routes to trade with the Mojave Indians who lived in California near the Colorado River. The Mojave Indians were the middlemen between their territory and inland and coastal tribes of Southern California. A **middleman** exchanges items with one group and then exchanges the trade item again with another group.

Trails also ran from the Pacific shore across the coast range mountains into the interior valley. Trails continued across the Sierra Nevada Mountains through the main passes, such as Carson Pass and Donner Pass, into the Great Basin of Nevada. Many of the routes the Indians used are still in use today. Parts of Highway 101 and 99 as well as other roads and highways follow the original Indian trails.[28]

A raccoon skin quiver for carrying arrows was highly prized as a trade item. Goods like this quiver could be traded again and again and be passed on for hundreds of miles.

The Indians who crossed the California deserts and mountains to trade with tribes in the valleys and along the coast, often stopped at a desert oasis to rest. The cool waters were refreshing and the native palm trees provided shade. Berry-like clusters of fruit that hung from the branches of the palm trees provided food.

INTERESTING THOUGHTS

Do you ever wonder how trading started between the Indian tribes of California? Here are some ideas. Perhaps the Hupa tribe had an extra large harvest of acorns and their neighbors, the Yuroks, had collected a large amount of dried seaweed. Knowing this, the tribes got together and exchanged acorns for seaweed. In the Chimariko tribe, the women might trade baskets with the Wintu women. While trading baskets, the Chimariko women might have noticed the beautiful red and black obsidian the Wintu men used to chip arrowheads. This could lead to the Chimariko men coming to the Wintu to trade for obsidian.

The Yokuts from the Northern part of the Great Central Valley on a trip to the coast, may have noticed large amounts of shellfish collected by the Ohlone Indians. Do you think the Ohlones would have traded dried shellfish for pinenuts that the Yokuts carried?

The Mojave traveled through the desert. Would they be carrying dried mesquite beans, gourds, and rabbit skins to trade for steatite with the Gabrielinos?

Because of the abundance and variety of the natural resources in California, trading became an important part of the lives of the Indians. Trading not only provided foods, goods, and an exchange of ideas, but it also strengthened friendships among people. Today tribal Gatherings and Big Times throughout California bring many people together for trading and selling goods such as baskets, arrowheads, and food. Most importantly these Gatherings include the sharing of ideas, friendships, dancing, and strengthening of family ties and traditions.

BACKTRACKING

Can you answer the following questions?

(1) Why was trading important to the California Indians?

(2) With whom did the Yuki trade? Using your California tribal map, name three tribes with whom the Yuki people might have traded.

(3) List three things the Yuki might have used as trade items.

(4) What items would the Yuki have received in exchange?

(5) The Southern California Indians traded for steatite. How was this soft stone used?

(6) Name five or more items most traded by the Indians throughout California.

(7) Name three kinds of trade money. Which kind of money was used throughout most of California?

(8) Explain the meaning of the following sentence: "On the longest trade routes the traders usually traveled only short distances, but the goods they carried could be passed on for hundreds of miles from where they started."

Vana Parrish Lawson is the nursery assistant at the Ya-Ka-Ama Indian Education & Development Center near Santa Rosa, California. Vana knows a great deal about native plants that were used by the Pomo Indians of California. When she was a young girl, Vana helped her mother, Essie Parrish, collect herbs and plants.

CHAPTER FOUR
NATURE'S NOURISHMENT

SEEDS, ROOTS, AND PLANTS

THE FIRST BOTANISTS

Nature's **nourishment** for the California Indians was a varied diet of acorns, native plants, deer, small animals, birds, and fish. The Indians gathered bulbs and tender plant shoots in the spring, seeds in the late spring and summer, and acorns, nuts, and berries in the fall. During the winter months, the food of the Indians consisted mainly of acorns, dried meat, seeds, and nuts. The Indians also traded with other Indian groups for food such as salt, dried or wet shellfish, and pinenuts. Foods were gathered for daily use, but most of the food was dried and stored for the winter. Thus, nature provided the Indians with year-round nourishment.

Among all the California Indians, the woman was the gatherer of all plant foods. In today's daily life she would be considered an expert **botanist**! She examined all plant foods carefully because she knew that she was responsible for the plant food needs of her entire family. If certain plants were not available during times of **drought**, the Indian woman knew other plants that could be **substituted**. She knew she had to gather the seeds and plants as well as prepare them for eating and storing. Can you imagine the patience an Indian woman must have had in order to accomplish this huge task?

THE MIGHTY OAK

Oak trees grew in most of California and the seed of the oak tree, called the acorn, provided most of the food for the California Indians. There are as many as eighteen **species** of oaks growing in California.[1] All of the acorns are **edible**, but some are better than others. Acorns contain starch, oil, sugar, and **citric** acid. Some are sweet, but many are bitter because they contain **tannic** acid.

There are two groups of oak trees—the white oaks and the red oaks. A third group of oaks called **intermediate** oaks may have the **characteristics** of either the white or red oak groups. The acorns of the white oaks are smooth inside and take one year to **mature**. The red oak acorns are furry inside and usually take two years to mature.[2]

Acorns were the most important food item among the Indians of California. Today many Indians throughout California continue to gather, store, and prepare acorns for their own use or for special ceremonies.

Valley Oak

GATHERING ACORNS

In the fall or autumn of the year, the Indians prepared to gather acorns. Acorns drop from the oak trees twice each fall. The first acorns that drop are often infested with worms and insects. The Indians do not gather these acorns. Later in the season, more acorns drop. These are the good acorns. The Indians gather the best acorns and leave the acorns with holes or cracks on the ground to be eaten by rodents and birds.

Most of the California Indians celebrated the coming of the acorn season with a special ceremony. At these ceremonies, families gathered together in prayer to thank the Great Spirit for the acorns. The Cahto Indians celebrated with an acorn dance. The Cahuilla had a special meal. The Hupa had an acorn feast. The Yuki sang about the acorns.[3] The Karuk began their year with the acorn harvest in the fall. They had a ten-day-long ceremony before the gathering of the acorns. The Kashaya band of the Pomo Indians ended their year in October with a thank you dance to the Great Spirit who had provided acorns and other foods throughout the year.[4]

Among some tribes, the harvesting of acorns was done mostly by women with the help of children. In other tribes such as the Pomo and the Wintu, men and boys helped the women gather the acorns.[5] The men and boys climbed the oak trees and knocked the acorns to the ground.[6] The women and children gathered the acorns in large burden baskets. Sometimes the Kashaya Pomo, the Sierra Miwok, and the Chumash used long sticks to knock acorns from the branches.[7] The average family could harvest the crop of an oak in one day. The hundreds of acorns gathered from one tree could amount to 140 pounds. The average family ate 500 to 800 pounds of acorns a year.[8]

Family groups worked together to collect acorns.

Indian families camped by the oak groves during the harvesting season. Sometimes, while they were camped in the oak groves, the men would hunt and the women would pound some of the acorns into meal. It was easier to carry acorn meal back to the villages than it was to carry heavy burden baskets of whole acorns. **Mortars** and **pestles** were used for pounding the acorns into meal. These stone tools were often left at the oak groves from year to year. The acorns that had not been pounded into meal were carried in burden baskets to the village to be stored for later use.

In some tribes such as the Tolowa, the Yurok, and the Kashaya Pomo, oak groves were owned by Indian families. If a tree did not produce acorns, the family leader would ask another family leader, whose trees had produced, if he could gather acorns from his trees.[9] Other tribes such as the Atsugewi, Achumawi, Yana, and Maidu shared gathering areas for acorns.[10]

There are more than 1200 holes in these mortar rocks at Chaw-se State Park in Pine Grove, California.

STORING ACORNS

Most of the acorns that were gathered in the fall were stored for the winter. Before the acorns were stored, they were dried to prevent molding. The acorns were spread out on mats or flat rocks to dry for a few weeks or a month.

The Indians built storehouses called **granaries** for the acorns. Here the acorns would be safe from rodents and birds. One type of granary was built off the ground, supported by a **framework** of small poles. The poles were usually covered with sticky **pitch** to prevent the rodents from entering the granary. The granary itself was made of tule or brush and often covered at the top with an animal skin to keep out moisture. In high altitudes granaries were made double thick to withstand snow.

The Indians of the south such as the Chemehuevi and Cahuilla, wove granaries from willow or other plant materials and placed them on pole-like legs or on top of high rocks. When an Indian woman wanted some acorns from the granary, she would pull apart the woven twigs near the base of the granary, making a small hole. When she had removed enough acorns from the granary, she would push the twigs back in place and close the hole. If a granary was more tightly woven, the woman would lift a tule or skin cover at the top to reach the acorns.

Other tribes, such as the Northern Maidu, stored extra acorns in holes dug into the sides of hills. The holes had been lined with pine needles. After the holes were filled, the acorns were covered with **cedar** bark and dirt. A long stick was also pounded into the ground to mark the location of the hole.[11]

Miwok Granary

Cahuilla Granary

PREPARING ACORNS

Indian women prepared the dried acorns for eating. The outer hard shells of the acorns were removed by cracking the shells with a firm tap from a **hammerstone**. The acorns were then placed in a **winnowing** basket and the thin skins on the acorns were winnowed off. The women used stone mortars and stone pestles to pound the acorn **kernels** into meal. Sometimes the women sat on large rocks and pounded the acorns in a hole in the rock. In many areas today you may still see mortar holes where Indian women once pounded acorns.

Using a hammerstone to remove the outer shell of the acorn

A winnowing basket is a flat, shallow basket used to separate the skin-like covering of the acorn from the kernel of the acorn. The winnowing basket was used to toss the acorn kernels into the air. As the acorns were tossed, the wind blew away the skin-like coverings from the acorns. Winnowing the coverings from the acorn kernels took much time.

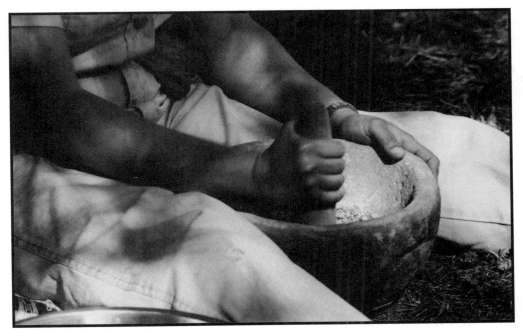

Using a mortar and pestle, the acorn meal is pounded into acorn flour.

The acorn meal had a bitter taste due to the natural tannic acid. This acid had to be **leached** out of the meal before the acorn meal could be used for food. The Indian women had ways to remove the tannic acid. Some women made a hollow in clean, hard packed sand by the side of a stream. In some mountain areas, the women lined this hollow with pine needles. The acorn meal was spread on the pine needles and fir boughs were placed across the acorn meal. Water was poured gently over the meal and allowed to trickle through to the sand. The water carried the tannic acid into the sand and left the acorn meal with a pleasant taste. If warm water was poured over the meal, it took less time to remove the tannic acid. When the sand had settled, the women would **skim** off the acorn meal and it was then ready to be used for soup, mush, or bread.

Cahuilla women leached the tannic acid from the acorn meal by using a loosely woven leaching basket. They lined the basket with a layer of grass or leaves. Then the meal was placed on the leaves. The leaves would keep the meal from being washed away. The same process of gently pouring warm or cold water over the meal was followed. Leaching tannic acid from acorn meal often took several hours, depending on the type of acorns used.

An Indian woman is removing the bitter tannic acid from the acorn meal before using it to make acorn mush.

When the acorn meal was ready, the women mixed it with water in a **watertight** basket. Then the meal was cooked by using a looped stick to place clean, hot stones from a campfire into the cooking basket. The heat from the hot stones made the water boil and cooked the acorn meal into mush. The mush was stirred constantly to keep the hot stones from burning the bottom of the basket. The stones were then removed and the mush was ready to eat. The cooking stones were carefully cleaned before and after each use.

Cooking stones were carefully selected. The Indians used a certain rock, rounded and fist-sized, that would not break or shatter when heated. Indian women would search the streams and river beds until they found just the right stones to be used for cooking.

In the desert areas, tribes such as the Mojave used pottery bowls directly over the fire to cook the acorn mush. Along the coast, steatite bowls were used by the Chumash Indians.[12]

Long ago an Indian woman had her digging sticks, her stirring paddles and looped sticks. Today's woman sometimes follows the ancient ways and uses a looped stick to put a hot rock into a basket of acorn mush. The rock will heat the acorn mush and cook it.

COOKING WITH ACORNS TODAY

Acorns continue to be an important part of the Indian culture. Acorn gathering today is usually not done with large burden baskets as used in the past. Boxes, bags, and sacks are used to collect acorns. The acorns may be dried in the sun or dried in ovens at a low temperature. Acorns may also be spread in low, flat cardboard boxes or trays and stacked and dried in a warm place. Dried acorns may be stored in cupboards or other storage areas.

Today when the acorns are ready to be used, the shells are sometimes cracked with a nutcracker or hammer. Husks are removed with the help of a small knife. The shelled and husked acorns are put in a coffee grinder, hand-turned meat grinder, or food processor and ground into meal. Leaching may be done with a strainer lined with cheesecloth or in a cheese-cloth sack attached to a water faucet. Cold water is run repeatedly over the flour until the meal loses its bitter flavor. After leaching, the acorn meal is used in bread, mush, cookies, pie crust, or pancakes. Acorn meal may be used to thicken stews and soups.

Cooking with acorns today takes time and effort. Modern methods such as using a nutcracker, coffee grinder, or leaching in a cheesecloth sack may shorten acorn making, but when acorns are prepared for special ceremonies, many California Indian women still use the old ways.[13]

Combining old ways and modern ways of leaching tannic acid from the acorn meal

A STORY FROM NORTHERN CALIFORNIA

The following story is called "The Acorn Maidens." It is told by the Karuk Indians of Northern California.

*THE ACORN MAIDENS

"It is said that once acorns were Yassaras (spirits). Life Givers came and told them, 'You are going to go. You must all have nice hats, but you must weave them.'

When they started to weave their hats, they said, 'We must all wear good looking hats.'

Then suddenly, Life Giver told them, 'You better go. Human is being raised.'

Black Oak Acorn had not finished her hat. She picked up her big pole basket. And Tan Oak Acorn did not clean her hat, and the uneven straw ends stuck out the side of her basket, so she just wore it wrong side out when she finished it.

The Post Oak Acorn just finished her hat out good. She finished it and cleaned it well.

Then Tan Oak Acorn said, 'Wouldn't I be the best acorn soup though my hat is not cleaned?'

Then they went. They spilled (from the heavens) into Human's place. Then they said, 'Human will spoon us up. They were Yassaras (spirits) too, but they were heavenly Yassaras.'

They shut their eyes and then turned their faces into their hats when they came to this earth here. That is the way the acorns did.

Tan Oak Acorn began to wish bad luck toward Post Oak Acorn and Maul Oak Acorn just because they had nice hats. She was jealous of them. They, in turn, wished her to be black.

continued

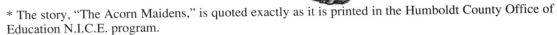

* The story, "The Acorn Maidens," is quoted exactly as it is printed in the Humboldt County Office of Education N.I.C.E. program.

Nobody likes to eat Post Oak Acorn and Maul Oak Acorn does not taste good either. Their soups are black and Maul Oak Acorn is too hard to pound.

They were all painted when they first spilled down. Black Oak Acorn was striped. When one picks it up off the ground nowadays, it is still striped.

Tan Oak Acorn was also striped, but she did not paint herself much because she was still mad. Because she said, "My hat is not finished."

When they spilled down, they turned their faces into their hats. And nowadays, they still have their faces inside their hats."

* * * * *

What do you notice about the acorns in this mortar?

As the Indian women pounded in the mortar, the sides of the bottomless baskets kept the acorn meal from flying out. Many Indians used mortars and pestles to pound acorns and seeds. Pounding tools are still used today. Mortars and pestles may be seen in museums. Some of these rocks have a black ring around them. This indicates that a bottomless basket was attached with asphaltum. Did you notice the acorns have not been shelled?

There were other important uses of the oak tree. Wood from this tree was very useful in making hot, long-lasting fire and considered one of the best materials for making wooden mortars. Oak wood and bark were burned and used in medicines. The oak gall, a fungus that sometimes grows on the oak tree, was pounded into a powder and used as a wash for the eyes or open sores. It was also mixed with deer brains, cooked and used for tanning hides.

AGAVE OR CENTURY PLANT

Acorns were the main staple food for the Indians throughout California. In Southern California, however, Indians such as the Mojave, Yuma, Cahuilla, Chemehuevi, Koso, and Tubatulabal used other important plant sources, one of them being **agave**, also called mescal or century plant.

Three parts of the agave were used—the flower, the leaves and the stalk. The flowers of the agave plant were gathered and boiled a few minutes to remove the bitter taste. They were eaten or dried for later use. The dried

Agave gathering areas were owned by families, just like some families owned acorn groves. Harvesting the broad, flat, cactus-like leaves was usually a man's job.

flowers could be stored for as long as five years. When the family was ready to use the dried flowers, the flowers were reheated in warm water.

The leaves were best when picked in the fall to spring months because they were tender and juicy. The leaves were baked and eaten or dried for later use.

The stalk of the agave was the most prized part of the plant. The stalk was best before it started to flower. When the stalk started to flower, it became **fibrous** and was not as tasty. Stalks were roasted in large underground pits. The roasted stalks were eaten or pounded into small patties and sun dried. These patties were stored for later use.

Indians could harvest agave in April and May, but the best time was in November and December. Harvesting the agave involved cutting down the whole plant—flowers, leaves, and stalks. The agave plant, however, is much like a banana tree. Even though most of the plant is destroyed in harvesting, it will still send out small, new, young shoots that will root and grow into new plants. As the agave matured, the plants had to be carefully watched because animals liked to nibble the sweet, tender leaves. The thorns of the agave were used like needles for tattooing. The fibers from the pounded leaves were used for cord, rope, sandals, nets, mats, snares, slings, and bowstrings.[14]

MESQUITE, ANOTHER IMPORTANT BASIC FOOD

Another main food source for the Cahuilla, Chemehuevi, Mojave, and other tribes of Southern California was the **mesquite**. These trees and shrubs grew in groves and like the agave and acorn, were useful in many ways. The Indians ate the blossoms in the spring, the green bean pods in the summer, and the dried pods in the fall.

The flowers were picked and roasted in a pit with heated stones. Next they were squeezed into balls and stored in pottery jars. When needed, they were cooked in boiling water. Sometimes, the flowers were made into tea.

The green bean pods were crushed in mortars made of mesquite wood. A stone or wooden pestle was used to pound the pods. The Cahuilla people made a refreshing summer drink by adding water to the crushed pods. The drink was stored in clay jars called **ollas**.

The dried pods, gathered in autumn, were eaten soon after picking or pounded into meal. Water was added to the meal. Later, when the meal had dried, it was formed into patties or cakes and allowed to harden. The mesquite cakes were stored for future use and were excellent for traders or hunters to take with them on long journeys.

Mesquite wood made hot fires and the wood was also used for making bows. The framework of some desert homes such as Cahuilla, was made from mesquite limbs. The limbs were also used for holding up large granaries. The thicker pieces of wood were made into mortars for pounding mesquite seeds into meal. The thorns of the mesquite were used to puncture the skin for tattoos.[15]

The Cahuilla women used the large boulders near the mesquite trees to pound the mesquite beans into meal. Water was added to the meal. When the meal dried, it was formed into small cakes and stored in baskets. Pieces were broken from these cakes and eaten dry or made into a mush.

PINENUTS

Pinenuts were gathered and prized by tribes throughout California. Pinenuts were collected in the fall and Indian families made long journeys into the mountains to gather them. The Indians knocked the pinecones from the pine trees and removed the nuts from the pinecones. When pinenuts were collected, a winnowing basket was used to separate the nuts from small twigs. The nuts were then roasted by putting them in a basket with hot coals. The basket and nuts were shaken so that the coals would not burn the basket and the nuts were well roasted. Then the shells were cracked with a stone. Again the winnowing basket was used to separate the nutmeats from the ashes left by the hot coals. Often an Indian woman said a silent prayer to the winds to help her with the winnowing.

Pinenuts were also eaten raw, boiled into a mush or pounded and made into cakes. Paiute Indians gave their babies a thin mush made from pinenuts. Pinenuts are rich in protein and fat and were a welcome addition to the Indian's diet.

Today, the pinenut is still important in the lives of many Indians. In the fall, families travel to the Sierra Nevada Mountains to gather pinenuts from the Pinyon tree. They take ladders for climbing the trees, hooked poles for knocking and pulling down cones, and canvas and sheets for collecting the fallen nuts. Plastic buckets and boxes take the place of burden baskets. Old and young go by truck high into the Sierras sometimes to camps that have been used by generations of Indians. Today, binoculars are sometimes used to find the Pinyon trees with the most cones. When the first cones are knocked to the ground, the nuts are tasted and the group gathers together in prayer to thank the earth for her gifts. After the pinenuts are gathered, they are shelled and roasted or eaten raw. Gathering together to collect pinenuts keeps the old ways alive and links the present with the past.[16]

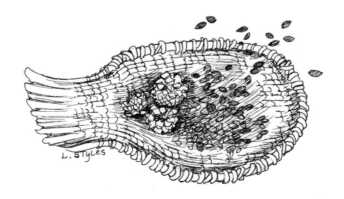

A PAIUTE PRAYER

*Paiute Pinenut Prayer

"When we come to a pinenut place we talk to the ground and mountain and everything. We ask to feel good and strong. We ask for cool breezes to sleep at night. The pinenuts belong to the mountain so we ask the mountain for some of its pinenuts to take home and eat. The water is the mountain's juice. It comes out of the mountain, so we ask the mountain for some of its juice to make us feel good and happy. Just the old people do this. The young people don't care; they just walk on the mountain anyhow."

HARVEST TIMES

Harvesting seasons for acorns, agave, mesquite, and pinenuts were special occasions for the Indians. Friends and relatives who had not seen each other for several months, camped side by side and listened to each other's stories of births, deaths, marriages, and other recent happenings among the tribes. These times also were **courting** times for young men and women.

SOME INDIANS PLANTED CROPS

Most of the California Indians did not grow green vegetables, but they did have green plants in their diet. They gathered nettle, wild onions, bracken greens, Indian or miner's lettuce, and many other green plants. Most of the Indians did not grow crops because they were skilled gatherers of nature's gifts that grew **abundantly** in all of California. The Indian women gathered seeds, roots, plants, flowers—every type of plant that could be used as food. What they did not eat immediately, they dried and stored for winter use. The Indians respected nature and gave thanks to the Great Spirit whenever they gathered food. They never gathered more than their family or tribe could use.

*The poem, "Paiute Pinenut Prayer," is quoted exactly as it is printed in the book entitled **Survival Arts of the Primitive Paiutes** by Margaret M. Wheat, published by the University of Nevada Press.

There is evidence, however, that Indians in parts of Southern California grew crops long before the non-Indians came. The Indians along the Colorado River grew squash and pumpkins and the overflow from the river watered their crops. The squash and pumpkins were boiled or roasted in a fire and the seeds were sun-dried for winter use.

Few tribes planted crops, but many tribes practiced burning the fields and meadows. The Indians knew that burning would remove unnecessary plants or brush on the land. The ashes from the burning enriched the soil so that the following season the young plants grew stronger. The Indians learned about burning by observing nature at work. When lightning caused a fire and land was burned, the Indians noticed that the following season's plant growth was more **productive** than usual. And so, the Indians learned that by controlled burning of grasslands, they could look forward to a more abundant food supply.[17]

OTHER NATIVE PLANTS USED BY THE INDIANS

On the following pages, you will find pictures, descriptions and uses of some native plants used by the California Indians. When you come to the conclusion of each plant description, you will notice how, today, we use these same plants that the Indians discovered and put to use long before non-Indians came.

Before you read about the following plants used by the Indians, you should understand that eating any of the plants without properly identifying them could be very DANGEROUS! Never eat any plant without first checking with a knowledgeable person.

* * * * *

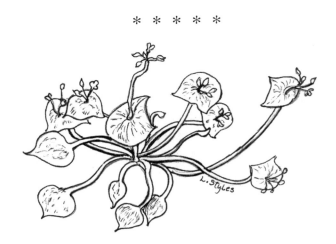

ANGELICA

DESCRIPTION

This stout plant grows one to four feet high and is related to the celery family. The leaf stalks have leaves in groups of three.

HABITAT

Angelica grows on the plains and high in the mountains.

INDIAN USES

The Huchnom Indians of Northern California used Angelica as a cough medicine. The Hupa Indians as well as other tribes used this plant in many ways. The Hupa medicine people burned Angelica in a fire while making spiritual medicine.

The root is dried, used in pipes and smoked in ceremonies. The dried root is used on cuts and sores and sometimes brewed into a strong tea for people who were very ill. Poultices were made from this plant and used for rheumatic pains. The Kashaya Pomo used Angelica as a cure-all plant. They also ate the young shoots, but after the plant leafed out, it was no longer eaten.

USES TODAY

Angelica is still used in some Indian ceremonies. It is very important in Hupa ceremonies.[18]

ARROWHEAD
TULE POTATO

DESCRIPTION

The Arrowhead plant stands one to three feet in height. It has long arrow-shaped leaves with flowers that come from the top of the stem and stand higher than the leaves. The flowers are white with gold or green centers.

HABITAT

This plant grows in wet marshy areas, ponds, and fresh water river edges. It grows throughout California below 7000 feet.

INDIAN USES

The roots were eaten raw, roasted, or boiled. The roots were dried and pounded into flour.

USES TODAY

The roots make excellent outdoorsman food for they are used just like a potato.[19]

**BEAVERTAIL
PRICKLY PEAR**

DESCRIPTION

The Beavertail is a cactus with flat, fleshy joints or pads. It grows in clumps with fine short spines. Large, waxy flowers appear on the cactus in the spring. The fruit that forms on the cactus is reddish, pear shaped, and very juicy.

HABITAT

This cactus grows in the Mojave and desert areas of Southern California.

INDIAN USES

The large fleshy joints or pads were split and scraped and used as a wet dressing to help reduce swelling and deaden the pain from bites or wounds. The fruit and young fleshy joints (with the spines removed) were dried in the sun, then boiled and eaten. The young fruits were also cooked in stone lined pits for 12 hours. In the Panamint Mountains, the Indians used not only the young fruits, but dried the flower buds and the young fleshy joints.

USES TODAY

The fruit can be eaten raw or made into jelly or pickles. The young fleshy joints or pads are cooked and used as a vegetable.[20]

BARBERRY
OREGON GRAPE
MOUNTAIN GRAPE

DESCRIPTION

The Barberry is a tall bush with bright green, crisp leaves. It has yellow flowers that blossom in the spring.

HABITAT

The Barberry is found on the wooded slopes of California below 4000 feet. It is found from San Diego to Oregon in the lower mountains.

INDIAN USES

The roots and bark were used to heal sores and were also used to treat heartburn and rheumatism. The bark and roots were made into a yellow dye for baskets. The Karuk Indians used the plant dye to decorate bows and arrows.

USES TODAY

Tea is made from the roots and used as a diuretic and laxative. Jelly is made from the berries.[21]

BEARGRASS

DESCRIPTION

Beargrass has long, slender leaves growing upward from the bulb with small white flowers that form clusters. The leaves and stalk are very slippery. Beargrass is also called Bear Lily, Pine Lily or Elk Grass, and Turkey Beard.

HABITAT

The plant grows on mountain slopes and high open forests of Northern California. It grows at altitudes of 6000 feet and below.

INDIAN USES

Parts of the plant were dried and bleached and the fibers were used for white patterns in baskets. Northern and Central Indians used fibers split from the leaves as white overlay in their basketry.

USES TODAY

Fibers from the plant are used in basketmaking today.[22]

BRACKEN FERN

DESCRIPTION

The Bracken Fern grows one to four feet high and toothlike leaves grow from the stalks.

HABITAT

The fern grows in ponds, streams, open woods, and meadows. It grows throughout California and is the most abundant fern growing in the Sierra Nevadas.

INDIAN USES

The Yurok and other Indians of Northern California boiled and ate the starchy root. In the spring the young tender curled tips were used as a green vegetable.

USES TODAY

The young curled ferns are eaten raw in salads, cooked as a vegetable, or baked in casseroles.[23]

CALIFORNIA BAY
CALIFORNIA LAUREL

DESCRIPTION

The California Bay tree grows fifty to one hundred feet high. It has dark green leaves that give off a strong odor when crushed. The flowers are greenish yellow. The small round nuts turn dark purple.

HABITAT

These trees are found along streamsides and in woodlands and valleys. They grow below 5000 feet from San Diego to Oregon.

INDIAN USES

Many tribes used the leaves for medicine. The leaves were bound to the forehead or placed in the nostril to cure headaches. The leaves were also bound around the stomach to cure stomach aches. The leaves were used as a flea repellent or sometimes burned in the home when someone had a cold. The nuts were roasted, cracked, and pounded into small cakes.

USES TODAY

The leaves are placed in chicken houses to prevent lice and when hung with garlic to dry, they prevent molding. The leaves are also used in cooking.[24]

CALIFORNIA BLACKBERRY
PACIFIC BLACKBERRY
BRAMBLE BUSH

DESCRIPTION

The California Blackberry is a thorny, trailing shrub and often grows into large bushes.

HABITAT

The California Blackberry can be found from California to Canada. It grows beside streams and ponds where it is damp and moist.

INDIAN USES

The Indians picked the berries that ripened in the summer and early fall. They ate them fresh or dried the berries for later use. Most of the time the berries were mashed and poured into flat baskets to dry. In the winter these slabs of blackberries were broken into pieces and eaten. The Indians of Northern California made a tea from the roots that was used to treat diarrhea. The Cahuilla Indians of Southern California soaked the berries in water to make a pleasant drink.

USES TODAY

The berries are eaten fresh and are used in many desserts. They are also used to make jelly, jam, and tea.[25]

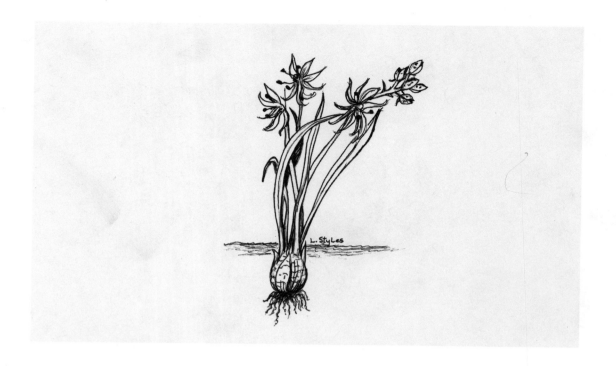

CAMAS

DESCRIPTION

The stalk of the Camas plant grows two feet high with small dark blue blossoms.

HABITAT

The Camas grows in moist ground and is found in meadows and among pine forests. In the Coastal Mountain ranges, Camas grows from Marin County to the Sierra Nevadas and from Mono County to Tulare County.

INDIAN USES

Camas was a very important Indian plant food. The Atsugewi, Lassik, and other Indian tribes baked, boiled, or pounded the Camas bulbs into meal. The cooked bulbs were pressed into thick brown cakes or sometimes boiled down into a thick molasses. The cooked bulbs are said to have the flavor of a chestnut.

USES TODAY

Bulbs are cooked.[26]

CASCARA TREE OR SHRUB

DESCRIPTION

Cascara trees or shrubs have smooth gray, brownish bark, dark green oblong shaped leaves, and round black berries. The California Coffee Berry is a close relative of the Cascara.

HABITAT

These trees grow in Northwestern California in the Pacific Coast mountains.

INDIAN USES

Of all the plant medicines used by the Indians, Cascara was one of the best known. The outer bark was peeled and dried. Later it was soaked and boiled for an hour. The liquid was used as a laxative.

USES TODAY

Cascara is used as a natural laxative in medicine today and can be found in health food stores.[27]

CATTAIL

DESCRIPTION

Cattail plants are three to seven feet tall with long, slender leaves and sausage shaped catkins.

HABITAT

Cattails are found in ponds, streams, and marshlands of California.

INDIAN USES

Cattails were used by many Indian tribes in California. The roots were eaten raw or roasted and the young roots were considered a delicacy. The root was also peeled, dried, pounded, and used as flour. The pollen from the catkin was mixed with water and made into cakes, mush, or bread. The fluff from the spike of the cattail was used to line cradle boards and used as a diaper for babies.

USES TODAY

The tender, inner leaves are gathered and eaten as a snack or put in salad.[28]

L. Styles

CEANOTHUS

DESCRIPTION

The Ceanothus is a small tree or shrub, two to twenty feet high. It is evergreen with tiny leaves. The flowers bloom white to blue and have a spicy odor.

HABITAT

The Ceanothus is found on open slopes, woodlands, and coastal areas throughout California.

INDIAN USES

The bark and roots were brewed as a tea and used as a tonic, while the leaves were sometimes smoked as tobacco. The Ceanothus seeds were eaten. The red roots gave a red dye and the blossoms were rubbed on the skin as a wash for rashes.

USES TODAY

Parts of the plants are used in many medicines—blood coagulant, stimulant for getting rid of mucous, and a liver and spleen medicine.[29]

CHIA

DESCRIPTION

The Chia plant grows three to fifteen feet high with small blue flowers and gray-green leaves. The brown stalks have clusters at the top where hundreds of tiny, black seeds are formed.

HABITAT

Chia grows over a large part of California below 4000 feet. It may be found in woodlands and grasslands.

INDIAN USES

The Indians gathered the nutritional seeds and ground them to be cooked later as mush or soup. One teaspoon of the dried seeds would give an Indian enough energy for 24 hours! A strong tea made from parts of the plant was used as a stomach medicine or to relieve soreness or infection of the eyes. Seeds were sometimes stirred into the water to neutralize the alkaline water of the desert water holes.

USES TODAY

The seeds are sold in health food stores and are sprouted and used in salads or sandwiches. The seeds can also be made into a tea or stirred into lemonade to make a refreshing drink.[30]

CREOSOTE BUSH

DESCRIPTION

Creosote Bush is a strong scented bush with yellow flowers that bloom in April and May.

HABITAT

The Creosote Bush is found in desert areas and on dry slopes from Southern California to Kern County and up to about 5000 feet.

INDIAN USES

The Cahuilla Indians and other tribes of Southern California made a tea from the stems and leaves to help relieve colds, infection, coughs, and stomach problems.

USES TODAY

A drug is being produced from the Creosote Bush to keep butter, bacon, and fats from spoiling. Cahuilla and other Indians today boil the leaves in a pot and inhale the steam to help colds and coughs.[31]

ELDERBERRY

DESCRIPTION

The Elderberry is a shrub or a small tree with cream-colored scented flowers. Small, blue or black berries appear in September.

HABITAT

The Elderberry grows in open areas and valleys at lower elevations.

INDIAN USES

Throughout California the Indians used the blossoms to make a tea to treat fevers, colds, and upset stomachs. A wash made from elderberries and water was used to treat wounds. Stems were used for arrowshafts, whistles, flutes, and clapsticks. Dye from the fruit and twigs was used for basketry. Berries were used in several ways, for a drink and also dried and stored for winter use.

USES TODAY

The clusters of small blossoms are picked, dipped in batter and deep fried. The berries are used to make jam, jelly, and pies.[32]

FREMONTIA
FLANNEL BUSH

DESCRIPTION

The Fremontia is a scraggly shrub or tree growing from six to twenty feet tall. The leathery dark green leaves are fuzzy underneath and yellow, saucer-like flowers grow in May and June. The seed capsules are covered with bristly, rust colored hairs.

HABITAT

The Fremontia grows throughout California on hillsides and in dry areas.

INDIAN USES

The fiber from the bark was sometimes twisted into string and the smaller branches were used for making bows and arrows. The slippery inner bark was used for poultices. Sometimes the bark was brewed into a tea for irritations of the throat.

USES TODAY

The Fremontia is used in drought areas and along highways as a decorative plant.[33]

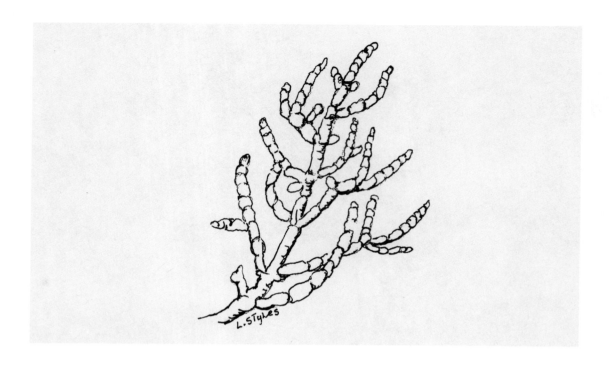

GLASSWORT
SALTWORT

DESCRIPTION

Glasswort is a fleshy herb with jointed branched stems. It has no leaves. In the summer the stems are bright shiny green and in the autumn the stems are yellow-orange and red.

HABITAT

This plant grows in salt marshes along the coastline from Central California to Lower California.

INDIAN USES

The Indians ate Glasswort raw and enjoyed the salty taste. The leaves were gathered, boiled, and eaten as greens. They dried it and traded it. The seeds of Glasswort were gathered by the Cahuilla Indians and pounded into flour.

USES TODAY

Glasswort can be added to salad or made into pickles.[34]

**INDIAN HEMP
DOGBANE**

DESCRIPTION

Indian Hemp grows three to four feet tall. It is a stout plant and grows stiff and tall with branches near the top.

HABITAT

Indian Hemp is found below 5000 feet throughout most of California. It grows as a weed and in moist places near streams.

INDIAN USES

Indian Hemp was well known among the California Indians as a source of fiber. Long strips of fiber were scraped from the stems of the plants. The fiber was made into string for fishing and carrying nets as well as rope.

USES TODAY

Indian Hemp is used in weaving tump lines and rope.[35]

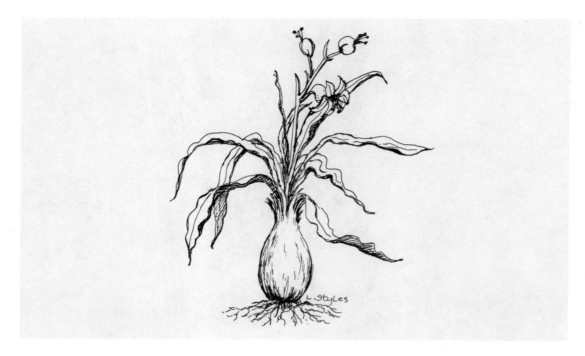

DESCRIPTION   **INDIAN SOAP ROOT**

Indian Soap Root grows two to three feet tall with long narrow fluted leaves. The flowers have white petals with green veins. The fiber-covered bulb grows underground.

HABITAT

The Indian Soap Root can be found growing on hillsides, in valleys and woodlands, grasslands and by streams.

INDIAN USES

The Hupa Indians and most tribes throughout California used the crushed bulb of the Soap Root to stupefy fish in rivers and streams. Brushes were made from the brown outer fibers of the bulb. Glue was made from the crushed and cooked bulb of the Soap Root. Layers of this glue were molded around one end of the tightly wrapped fibers of the brush to form a handle. The crushed bulb was used also as a shampoo and when baked the bulb was edible. The gluey substance that oozed from the bulb during baking was used by the Indians to glue feathers to arrowshafts.

USES TODAY

The heavy brown fibers that cover the bulb are taken off the bulb, washed, combed, and put back together to form a brush. Many layers of Soap Root glue are put on the upper part of the fibers of the brush and made into a handle. The handles can also be covered with charcoal blackened pine pitch.[36]

JIMSON WEED
STINKWEED

DESCRIPTION

Jimson Weed is a beautiful, but very poisonous plant. It has long bell-shaped white flowers and bright green leaves. The leaves smell like rancid peanut butter and so the plant is also called stinkweed.

HABITAT

Jimson Weed grows in dry places over most of Southern California and as far north as the Sacramento Valley.

INDIAN USES

A brew was made from the crushed seeds and roots which was used in special ceremonies. The leaves were smoked by most of the tribes in the south for ceremonies. The crushed plant could be used on bruises, swellings, and bites.

USES TODAY

The plant is used for medicinal purposes as a prescribed drug.[37]

MANZANITA

DESCRIPTION

This shrubby evergreen plant has small, dark green leaves and reddish brown bark. It has tiny red berries from June to late fall.

HABITAT

Manzanita grows in oak woodlands and in pine forests.

INDIAN USES

The Mountain Miwok and other tribes ate the berries raw or dried them for winter use. They sometimes crushed the ripe berries and mixed them with water for a refreshing drink or made them into a thick jellylike mush. The leaves were made into a tea for curing diarrhea. Leaves were sometimes mixed with tobacco for smoking.

USES TODAY

The Miwok Indians make Manzanita cider. The stems are winnowed or picked off the ripe berries. Then the berries are crushed, soaked in warm water, and strained to make cider.[38]

MILKWEED

DESCRIPTION

Milkweed is a tall slender plant two to five feet tall with long narrow leaves. The stems have a milky juice when crushed.

HABITAT

This plant is found throughout California in fields, meadows and woodlands.

INDIAN USES

The California Indians used Milkweed in many ways. One of the most important uses of the Milkweed was to supply tough fibers for making cord and rope. The Indians removed and dried the outer fibers from the stalk. These fibers were made into string and fishnets. The milky juice from the plant was used for cuts, wounds, warts, and for tattooing. Sometimes it was hardened and used for chewing gum. The young leaves were used as greens and the roots were boiled for eating.

USES TODAY

The young shoots and buds from the milkweed are cooked or eaten raw in salads. Sometimes the milky juice from this plant is used to cure warts and to treat ring-worm.[39]

MINER'S LETTUCE

DESCRIPTION

This dainty looking plant grows six to twelve inches tall. The leaves are a roundish shape and encircle the stem. Above the stem, growing out of the center of the leaf, are clusters of pink or white flowers.

HABITAT

Miner's lettuce is found in mountain and coastal pine forests as well as oak woodlands and is usually found in damp, shady places.

INDIAN USES

The tender leaves were eaten green or cooked. A tea was made and used as a laxative. Some Indians picked the plant and placed them near a red ant nest. They let the ants crawl over the leaves and then shook the plants clean. A residue tasting like a vinegar salad dressing would remain.

USES TODAY

The greens are picked and used in salads.[40]

NETTLE

DESCRIPTION

Nettle grows from two inches to seven feet tall. The leaves grow opposite one another on a single stalk. The leaves are oblong with a heart shaped base and serrated edges. The older stalks and the under part of leaves have stinging bristles filled with fluid.

HABITAT

These plants are found throughout California in meadows, fields and woodlands.

INDIAN USES

Throughout California most of the Indians used Nettle. The young Nettles were gathered and boiled or eaten raw. The young Nettles are rich in vitamins and minerals. Parts of the plant were brewed into a tea and used for chest colds and internal pains. The Kashaya Pomo used Nettle for arthritis. They would hit the aching area with the stems of the plant. This treatment helped the patient for two or three days. Fibers from the plant were woven into cord and thread and used for bow strings and in basketmaking.

USES TODAY

The young greens are eaten raw in salads or cooked as a vegetable. The fiber is used in material, cording, or paper.[41]

SEAWEED
BROWN KELP

DESCRIPTION

Brown or Red Seaweed also known as Kelp, can grow as long as seventy-five feet. The Red Seaweed has fine mosslike leaves and the Brown Seaweed has wide coarse leaves.

HABITAT

These Seaweeds grow in the sea along the coast of California.

INDIAN USES

The Chumash, Pomo, and other Coastal Indians gathered and dried the Seaweed for use in cooking. It was a valuable trade item because it contained salt.

USES TODAY

Kelp is harvested to make fertilizers and explosives. Chemists extract a large amount of iodine and algin from Kelp. Algin is important because it can hold liquids together and is used in milk, ice cream, salad dressing, chocolate, and aspirin. Kelp is also dried and eaten.[42]

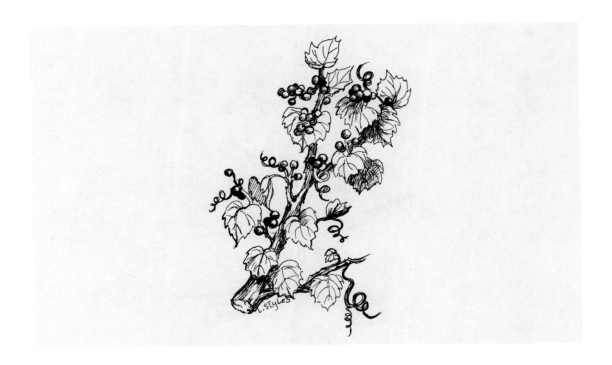

WILD GRAPE

DESCRIPTION

Wild Grape is a vine that grows five to sixty feet long. It bears small clusters of fruit, has large green leaves, and curly tendrils. The flowers are small and greenish white.

HABITAT

The Wild Grape is found in moist, fertile ground throughout California along streams, canyons, and in woodlands.

INDIAN USES

Some Indians used the wiry branches in twined basketmaking and for tying things together. The fruit was eaten fresh or dried and stored for winter use. The Indians ate the leaves and young tender green shoots. Sometimes the leaves were used as a poultice for snakebites.

USES TODAY

Fresh fruit is used for eating, dried for raisins, boiled for jelly, and crushed and fermented for wine. The young leaves are used in cooking.[43]

WILD IRIS

DESCRIPTION

Wild Iris is a small green plant that grows about one to two feet tall. It has long narrow leaves. The flowers look like small lilies and range in color from light to dark purple.

HABITAT

Wild Iris grows along the Pacific Coast from Santa Barbara to Oregon in Coastal areas and woodlands.

INDIAN USES

Wild Iris leaves were gathered and a single silky fiber was taken from each side of the leaf. None of the other fibers were used. Using a mussel shell, the women cleaned these fibers. The fibers were twisted into strong thread, cord and rope. This was a long process. The thread and cords were made into fishing nets and carrying nets as well as snares for catching deer, birds, and other game.

USES TODAY

Growing in its native habitat, Wild Iris is a very decorative plant.[44]

WILD ONIONS
BRODIAEA

DESCRIPTION

The Wild Onion has green, slender tubular leaves and stems. The onion bulb grows below ground and has a distinct strong odor. The flowers grow in umbrella shaped clusters of pink and white.

HABITAT

Wild Onion is found in moist ground throughout the west near streams, marshlands and meadows.

INDIAN USES

The Indians ate the Wild Onion bulbs raw or roasted. They dried and tied the onions into bundles for winter use. The whole plant was used as an insect repellent by rubbing it on the body and sometimes the bulb was pounded into pulp, mixed with animal fat, and used on snakebites.

USES TODAY

Onions are roasted, boiled, baked, and eaten raw. They are made into cough syrup and sometimes poultices are made from them.[45]

WILD ROSE

DESCRIPTION

The Wild Rose is a scraggly plant that grows three to six feet high. It has pretty pink blossoms. A rose hip (seedpod) forms beneath each blossom.

HABITAT

The Wild Rose is found near streams and rivers.

INDIAN USES

The Indians brewed a tea from the rose hips. The older wood was used for arrow-shafts.

USES TODAY

The rose hips are an excellent source of vitamin C and may be found in health food stores. They may be eaten raw or made into tea. The hips are also ground and used in vitamin pills. The rose petals are used raw in salads.[46]

WILD TOBACCO

DESCRIPTION

Tobacco is an herb that grows from one foot to five feet tall. The small, narrow leaves have a strong odor and are poisonous. The trumpet shaped flowers are white to greenish white.

HABITAT

Tobacco grows throughout a large part of California in washes, dry plains and open valleys. It grows below 8000 feet.

INDIAN USES

The Karuk Indians and other tribes dried and smoked the leaves for ceremonies. The leaves were sometimes crushed and made into poultices for bites and cuts.

USES TODAY

Wild Tobacco leaves are dried and used in California Indian ceremonies.[47]

WILLOW

DESCRIPTION

Willow trees and bushes come in many varieties. Salix willows have long green dark pointed leaves and grow twenty to thirty feet in height.

HABITAT

This tree is found throughout California near streams and in other moist areas.

INDIAN USES

The Indian women gathered parts of the Willow for basketmaking. The Luiseno Indians of Southern California used the pliable wood for bows. Willow wood was used for frames of homes. Fiber from the bark of the Willow was used for nets and clothing. The bark was made into a tea to relieve headaches, fever, aches, and pains of rheumatism. Some varieties of Willow produced seedpods that could be eaten.

USES TODAY

Salicylic acid is extracted from the Willow and used in many medicines, especially aspirin. Indian women and men of many tribes use Willow in their basketweaving.[48]

YERBA SANTA
MOUNTAIN BALM

DESCRIPTION

Yerba Santa is a shrub that grows two feet to eight feet tall. The leaves have a shiny surface but are fuzzy underneath. The dark lavender to white flowers grow in clusters on tiny stalks.

HABITAT

Yerba Santa grows throughout California on dry rocky slopes and in pine forests.

INDIAN USES

The leaves were boiled in a tea for many different illnesses such as coughs, colds, sore throats and rheumatism. The Miwok and Yuki put crushed leaves on their arms and legs to relieve pain. The Kashaya Pomo used Yerba Santa for congestion in the chest or for asthma. A tea was made from the leaves and the Indians drank the tea.

USES TODAY

The dried leaves are brewed for tea.[49]

YUCCA

DESCRIPTION

Yucca is a tall shrub that grows to the height of eighteen feet. It has thickly clustered, sharply pointed leaves. The bell-shaped flowers grow on a long stalk.

HABITAT

Yucca is found near desert scrub, chaparral or brush.

INDIAN USES

The flowers, stalks, and fruits were eaten by the Indians. The roots were used as soap and the fibers from the plant were used to make brushes. The Yucca was among the most valuable plants used by Southern California Indians such as the Mojave, Koso, Cahuilla, Chemehuevi, and Serrano.

USES TODAY

The fibers from the plant can be made into burlap, twine and rope. The root is used in commercial shampoos. The Yucca is a natural food remedy for arthritis. The fruits and flowers are used in cooking.[50]

INTERESTING THOUGHTS

Now that you have read about some of the native plants, seeds, and roots that the California Indians used, you may wish to ask your parents, grand-parents, or great-grandparents about some of these plants. Perhaps your grandparents might know of other plants that were used for food or medi-cine.

Plants such as mugwort, curly dock, clover, and wild mustard were brought to America by non-Indians. Your grandparents may remember hav-ing a mustard plaster put on their chests when they had a bad cold. Sometimes thick onion syrup was given for coughs. Sweet cascara bark was chewed as a laxative and is still used today in many types of medicines.

The Indians knew the use of every plant, seed, and root growing in California. They valued their land and every growing thing that the Great Spirit had created for them.

BACKTRACKING

Can you answer the following questions?

(1) Name some of the major sources of plant foods for the Indians in Northern California.

(2) Name some of the major sources of plant foods for the Indians in Southern California.

(3) How were acorns collected and stored?

(4) How were acorns prepared for eating?

(5) What Indian groups grew pumpkins and squash? How did these vegetables get water?

(6) Name four native plants and their medicinal uses.

(7) Why were Soap Root and Willow plants so popular with the Indians?

On the Klamath River, a Karuk Indian is fishing for salmon from a fishing platform. A basket cap on his head helps support the twelve-foot poles on his dip net. The area where he is fishing is known as "Amaikiara" in Northwestern California. The picture was taken in the year 1907.

CHAPTER FIVE
NATURE'S NOURISHMENT

HUNTING AND FISHING

Indian women were responsible for the gathering of acorns, seeds, nuts, and plants for the nourishment of their families. The men did the hunting and fishing. They hunted both large and small animals. Deer, antelope, desert sheep, elk, rabbits, and squirrels were some of the animals hunted for food in California. In the spring some tribes such as the Achumawi hunted large groundhogs or marmots.[1] Although many of the Indians of California did not hunt or kill bears, it is known that the Atsugewi Indians killed grizzly bears for food. The Karuk Indians who also hunted bears for food, killed bears that were hibernating in caves.[2] Some Pomo Indians as well as the Shasta, Coast Miwok, Yuki, and Maidu Indians also hunted bears.[3]

Many California Indians hunted the grizzly bear.

The Indians of California also hunted for quail, ducks, geese, pigeons, and doves. Birds were hunted with bows and arrows, snares, slings, clubs, baskets, and nets.

Many animals and birds were not eaten by certain tribes because they did not like the flavor of the food. Other tribes such as the Yurok, Atsugewi, and Yuki did not eat certain animals because of tribal customs. Some of these animals included marten, mink, gray fox, coyote, frog, eagle, buzzard, magpie, and crow.[4]

The Pacific Ocean, the rivers, and streams provided the Indians with a great variety of shellfish, salmon, eel, and trout. Salmon and trout were caught with spears, nets, traps, and dams. A crushed plant such as buckeye or soap root was sometimes dropped into quiet waters. This stunned the fish causing them to float to the surface where they were easily netted.[5] Members of tribes such as the Atsugewi, Achumawi, Yana, and Maidu often met on the Pit River to fish for salmon together.[6]

The Karkan Indians in the Carquinez Strait, near Martinez, California, baited animal flesh on a long, strong rope made of thick fibers. When a sturgeon or other large fish swallowed the bait, a barb would stick in the throat of the fish. Several Indians were sometimes needed to drag the fish from the water when it tired out. A sturgeon would sometimes be four to six feet long!

DEER HUNTING

Deer were hunted all year round. The Indians used bows and arrows to kill the deer and each man learned to make his own arrowheads, bows, arrowshafts, and quivers. The men took very good care of their hunting tools. Often one or two men of the tribe were so skillful at making arrowheads that they made all the arrowheads for the hunters. These expert craftsmen expected to share in a catch if the hunters brought back a deer.

The deer hunters prepared themselves **physically** as well as **spiritually** before each hunt. They lived in the **sweathouse** for several days and nights where they would sweat, **fast**, smoke, and dream. If the hunter had a dream about an animal the night before the hunt, it meant that he would be successful on the hunt.

On the day of the deer hunt, some Indian men rubbed herbs on their bodies to **disguise** their scent. Some Indians disguised themselves with deerskins and acted like deer so that they could creep close to their **prey** to shoot it with an arrow. In some tribes young men during their first year of hunting never ate any deer they killed for fear their luck would leave them.[7]

EXCELLENT ECOLOGISTS

After the hunt, the deer was brought back to camp and all parts of the animal were used. The antlers were used to chip obsidian into arrowheads, the leg bones were split and used for awls for piercing animal skins or making baskets, and the hoofs were used as rattles. The intestines were used as pouches and tying material, while the skins were used for clothing and blankets. The **sinew** was used for bowstrings. The head was cleaned and stuffed to be used as part of a hunting disguise when **stalking** deer, and the meat was roasted, stewed, or dried.[8]

We know that the Indians were excellent **ecologists**. When they went on a game hunt, they never killed more animals than they knew their tribe could use. When they killed any animal, the Indians always said a silent prayer to the animal's spirit so that the animal would be reborn. If the Indian did not take a deer during the hunt, then the wise hunter knew that the animal was not meant to die at that time.

The screech owl is the most common owl found in California and lives everywhere. The screech owl is not very large. It measures about eight inches in height and has a wing-spread of about twenty inches. This owl has big yellow eyes, eartufts that look like horns and a bad disposition. Owls are known for their silent flight, weird shrieks, and night travel. Many Indians feared owls because owls traveled at night and were associated with spirits and ghosts. Some Indians believed that an owl's call was to announce a spirit's arrival in the hereafter.

AN INDIAN STORY

The following story is from the Northern California Indians and is about an Indian woman who encouraged her husband to kill more owls than they really needed. She did not obey the Indian rule that the earth's gifts are not for the selfish or greedy.

* THE WOMAN WHO WAS NOT SATISFIED

"One time a man and his wife had been traveling for a great distance. Sun was going down to rest when they decided to camp in a cave until Sun woke and rose for the new day.

They were very hungry, but there was no food in the cave and that which they carried was gone.

As they made their fire, they heard the song of the horned owl a little way away from them.

* The story, "The Woman Who Was Not Satisfied," is quoted exactly as it is printed in the Humboldt County Office of Education N.I.C.E. program.

The wife turned to her husband and said, 'When Owl comes near, you can shoot him and we can eat him for supper.'

The husband then got his bow and his arrows which had the tiny obsidian points used for hunting birds. When he was ready, he sang out the same way as the owl.

Owl, thinking it was one of his cousins, returned the husband's call and came closer. The husband sang out again and when Owl answered the husband knew where Owl was, and he shot one of his arrows and being a good hunter, he had meat for his supper.

Then he said to his wife, 'There is enough for now.'

'No!' said the wife, 'We have had no meat for a long time. We shall want meat for tomorrow as well, for we have far to go. And if you call them when Sun comes up, they will not come.'

The man heard his wife and again taking his bow and arrows, called out for more owls. The husband began shooting his arrows as fast as the owls came. But there were more owls than arrows and still they came in great number.

Soon they covered everything, making Night Sky, filled with bright stars, darker than before. The husband covered his wife with a blanket and fought the owls with burning sticks from Fire. But there were too many. Then they overcame the husband and wife.

And this is the way the owls paid back the greedy husband and wife for the death of their cousins."

* * * * *

HUNTING SMALL GAME

Small game animals such as rabbits, squirrels, ducks, geese, quail, or woodpeckers were trapped and killed in several ways. Sometimes Indians shot pointed, sharpened sticks without arrowheads at rabbits and other types of small game. Rabbits were easily caught in nets, **snares**, or killed with a **throwing stick**.[9] The rabbits were skinned by the men and the women made blankets from the fur.

Quail and woodpeckers were sometimes caught in basket traps. Quail have poor eyesight, but good hearing. The Indians knew that the quail usually move uphill and so traps were set on slopes. The Indians walked quietly behind the quail and the **vibrations** of the Indians' feet would drive the frightened quail uphill into the trap. Once inside the basket trap, the quail could not find a way out. The Pomo Indians used quail traps as long as twenty-five feet.[10]

Sometimes basket traps were tied in place over woodpecker holes in trees. When the woodpecker came out of his hole, he was trapped in the long, narrow basket.[11] Other Indians such as Lake Miwok, Pomo, and Wappo used **slingshots** with rocks or clay balls to kill wild game such as ducks or geese. Slingshots were used by many California tribes.[12]

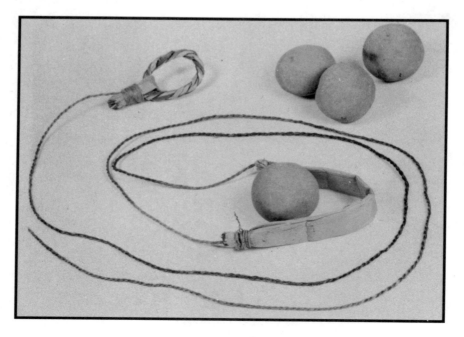

A Pomo sling made of green tule and milkweed fiber string

FISHING

Throughout California there are many lakes and rivers. Long ago, these lakes and rivers were abundantly filled with many kinds of fish. The Indians caught trout, steelhead, salmon, bass, sturgeon, perch, catfish, eel, and many other varieties of fish. Fishhooks made of shell or bone were mainly used when the Indians fished along the ocean shore or when fishing on lakes.[13]

Nets, spears, basket traps, and **weirs** were used in streams and rivers. Weirs or dams were made to catch salmon.[14] A weir is like a **latticework** dam made of **vertical** poles and cross pieces of branches. The poles were set like **tripods** to make the weir sturdy and then small branches were woven in and out of the poles to keep the salmon from getting through, except for one narrow opening. As the salmon swam through this narrow opening, the Indians were able to catch the fish by spearing them or by using dip nets. The Hupa were one of the tribes who used a weir or fish dam.[15]

Weirs were used in streams and rivers to catch salmon.

Basket traps for catching fish were large, coarsely woven baskets made so that the fish could swim in one end and not find their way out. Eels were also caught in this manner.[16]

Spears were used by every Indian in California who fished in large bodies of water. The long, slender spear shaft was good for jabbing. Some spear shafts, like arrowshafts, had a main shaft and a foreshaft. The foreshaft was usually double pronged, one prong being slightly longer than the other. Each prong had sharp **barbs** or points made of bone or flint and these barbs were glued to each foreshaft with pitch or asphaltum, then tightly wrapped with milkweed or iris fiber. The end of the fiber that held the barbs in place was then fastened to the main shaft of the spear. When the fish was speared, the foreshaft of the spear would detach, but the fiber that connected the foreshaft to the main shaft would allow the fisherman to pull the fish and foreshaft to shore.[17]

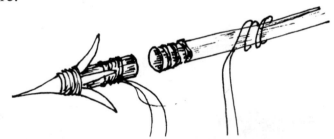

Many tribes used plants such as buckeye or soap root to paralyze the fish. These plants were pounded and scattered over the top of the water. The crushed plants would **paralyze** the fish and the fish would float to the surface of the water where the Indians would net them or scoop them out barehanded and throw them ashore. Tribes who fished in swift flowing rivers did not use buckeye or soap root to paralyze the fish. The fast moving waters washed the buckeye or soap root away before it could paralyze the fish.[18]

While the men fished, women cleaned and prepared the catch. They cut the fish into strips and dried them. They caught only as much fish as their families could use.

The Pomo Indians of the Clear Lake area often caught fish called hitch. The Indians cooked these fish for many hours in underground ovens. This long, slow cooking process softened the bones of the hitch so that the Indians could eat the entire fish, bones and all. Any extra amounts of fish were dried. Some of the dried fish, including the bones, was ground into a coarse meal. This fish meal could be stored for later use. The fish meal was used for soups and stews.[19]

SALMON AND LAMPREY EELS

The Hupa, Yurok, Karuk, Tolowa, and other Indian tribes fished for salmon and lamprey eels in the rivers of Northern California.

When the salmon traveled up the rivers from the ocean, the people held special ceremonies to celebrate the arrival of the salmon. The salmon lived in the ocean and swam up the rivers to lay eggs in the rivers where they were born. The Hupa Indians had a First Salmon Ceremony in the spring. Throughout the summer, the Indians speared the salmon or caught them in large nets. In September or October, the Indians built fish dams in the rivers for the fall salmon run. At this time there was another salmon ceremony.

Lamprey eels live in the rivers all year long. When young, the lamprey eels live in the calm, muddy river bottoms. After seven years they begin to grow eyes and tails. In a few months they grow into eels six to eight inches long. In the spring, when the eels go upriver to **spawn**, the Indians caught the eels with nets and traps. Special eel ceremonies were held in the spring.

The salmon and eels were roasted and eaten during the Salmon and Eel Ceremonies. Also, salmon and eel meat, as well as salmon eggs, were smoked and dried for winter storage. Today, Salmon and Eel Ceremonies are still an important part of the traditions of many Northern California Indian tribes.[20]

* * * * *

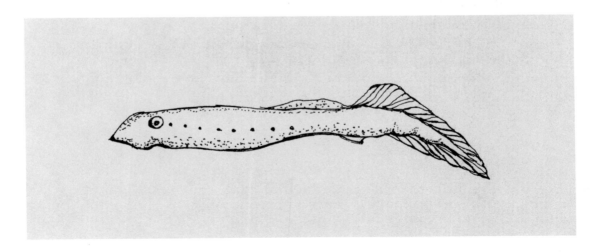

The Indians of Northern California used basket traps and nets to catch lamprey eels.

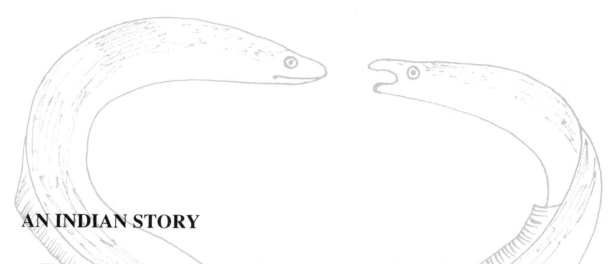

AN INDIAN STORY

The eel is a long snakelike fish without bones. In the following story the eel meets the sucker fish and you will find out how the eel loses its bones. The story is told by the Hupa, Karuk, and Yurok Indians.

*THE SUCKER AND THE EEL

"A long time ago, Eel and Sucker played a card game with sticks. Sucker was very, very lucky that day and Eel was very unlucky.

The two of them played their game until night and when they stopped, the Sucker had won all of the Eel's fine furs, all of his shell money, all of his best baskets, and even had won his house.

Eel was worried and sad. He sat thinking for a long time.

At last he said, 'Sucker, I'm going to play you one more game and I'll bet my bones I'll win this one.'

They played again, and again the Sucker won. That is why today Sucker has so many bones and Eel has none."

* * * * *

* The story, "The Sucker and the Eel," is quoted exactly as it is printed in the Humboldt County Office of Education N.I.C.E. program.

FOODS FROM THE SEA

The Indians who lived near the seacoast ate many varieties of seafood such as oysters, mussels, clams, barnacles, chitons, sea urchins, snails, crabs, abalone, octopus, sea bass, salmon, and sturgeon. These seafoods were usually roasted over fires or steamed in underground ovens. They were also dried and smoked for later use. As the Indians prepared and ate shellfish, they threw the shells in the same place until a mound or **midden** was formed from these shells. Sometimes other things such as tools, weapons, animal, and bird bones have been found in these shell mounds or middens.

Several hundred ancient village sites have been uncovered in the San Francisco Bay Area. There is a two-thousand-year-old shell midden in Coyote Hills Regional Park near Fremont, California that can be visited. Other Indian shell middens were located in Berkeley, San Mateo, the San Joaquin Delta, the Santa Barbara Channel, Humboldt Bay, San Diego, and in many other areas in California. Today, most of these shell middens have disappeared under the foundations of restaurants, beach-front homes, and landfill.[21]

The Chumash, Tolowa, and other tribes living along the coast used sea otters, seals and sea lions for food and skins. Men used boats to reach the offshore rocks where these animals rested. The hunters imitated the actions of the sea lions as they crept close enough to kill the animals. The dead animals were towed back to shore by boats. On land, the animals were skinned and prepared for cooking. Other times, the dead sea lions were skinned and cleaned on the rocks where they were killed. The meat was then packed into boats and taken to shore. The tusks of the sea lion were highly prized and used as necklaces or as ornaments on ceremonial **regalia**.[22]

This Hupa headband is made from the tusks of sea lions.

WHALES

Whales were frequently seen in the Pacific Ocean during certain periods of the year. These mammals were respected and known to the Indians. The California Indians did not go to sea to hunt these animals. We know that whales were used by the Indians because whale bones have been found in some of the coastal shell middens. Indians used whale meat from a whale that had grown weak or helpless and was washed ashore. Knowing that one of these huge mammals had been washed ashore was good news to the Indians living along the coast. The whale meat was roasted and eaten and extra meat was cut in strips and dried for winter storage.[23]

Whale meat was highly prized by the Indians. The meat is rich in oil and high in vitamins. Dried whale meat was often traded.

Snowy egrets were found among the marshlands and tules throughout California. The hollow leg bones of the heron and egret were used as whistles and flutes in dance ceremonies.

SEA BIRDS

Sea birds were also eaten by the Indians who lived along the coast. Some of these sea birds included sea gulls, cormorants, cranes, herons, pelicans, and terns.

Most sea birds lay their eggs in carefully built nests, but a few lay their eggs on ledges of rocks. Eggs supplied the Indians' diet with protein. Cormorant eggs were considered a **delicacy** by the Costanoan, Salinan, and Esselen tribes. At certain times of the year, Indians along the coast boated to offshore islands to collect these eggs.[24]

INTERESTING THOUGHTS

The Indians spent most of the year hunting, gathering, drying, preparing, and storing nuts, roots, seeds, meat, and fish for the long, cold months when their world would be caught in winter's grip. As the days grew shorter and the nights grew colder, the families gathered together in their homes near the heat of the fire. Occasionally, a person would rise to poke the fire and add more wood. The new firewood sparked and snapped and sent orange and black cinders drifting through the smoke hole in the roof of the home. The brightness from the newly stoked fire shone on the faces of the young and the old. Now was the time when the elders of the tribe told the creation stories. Everyone sat and listened to the elders tell the stories that had been told to them when they were young. After the long winter had passed, it was time once again to begin the gathering and collecting of nature's nourishment.

Long ago large herds of elk lived throughout California.

BACKTRACKING

Can you answer the following questions?
(1) Name five animals Indians hunted for food.

(2) What two animals did the Indians **not** kill for food? Why?

(3) Tell two ways the deer hunters prepared themselves before a hunt.

(4) What lesson or moral does the story "The Woman Who Was Not Satisfied" teach you?

(5) Name three ways Indians killed small game.

(6) What is a weir? How was it used by the Indians? Name two other ways Indians caught fish.

(7) Name three kinds of seafood eaten by the Indians living along the coast.

(8) What is a shell midden? Why are shell middens of importance to us today?

Basketry was once a very important part of native life of California. Today, basketry has become an Art Form. Here, Jennifer Bates, Northern Miwok, works on a basket at the California Indian Basketweavers Gathering. At the Gathering, Native California Basketweavers come together from all over the state to share their concerns and their art of basketmaking. Jennifer Bates is the Chairperson of the Board of Directors for the California Indian Basketweavers Association, CIBA. Photograph taken at the Tuolumne Rancheria in June, 1993.

CHAPTER SIX

USING NATURE'S GIFTS FOR BASKETS, BOWLS, AND BOATS

BASKETMAKING

Indians in all of North America made baskets, but the baskets made in California were especially fine. Basketmaking was more than just a part of daily life—it was and still is a very important part of California Indian culture. Baskets have been made by the California Indians since ancient times. Pieces and parts of baskets found in caves date back thousands of years.[1]

It is very hard to imagine how important basketry was in the daily lives of the California Indians. Indian women wove baskets for many purposes. There were baskets for cooking, storing food, carrying, winnowing, sifting, and games. They also wove beautiful gift baskets, often decorated with shells and feathers.

A small gift basket made by Myrtle McKay, 1993

Making baskets was a part of an Indian woman's life. As a young girl, she helped her mother, grandmother, or aunts collect and prepare materials for weaving baskets. As they gathered the grasses and shoots, the women thanked the Creator for providing the materials for basketmaking. The young girl watched carefully as the women spent long hours weaving fine baskets. For the young girl there would be hours of watching and many more hours of practicing. One day it would be time for the young woman to put the skills that she had learned into her own beautiful basket.

*AN INTERVIEW WITH MY GRANDMA
Alberta (Shosh) Sylvia
(well-known basketmaker)

SASHA: What do you use to make a basket?

SHOSH: We use hazel sticks. Mostly I use hazel sticks and some use willow sticks to make an open weave. By open weave I mean table mats, rattles, baby baskets, or flower vases.

SASHA: Where do you get your materials?

SHOSH: We go to get our hazel sticks after a burn the spring before. Then we will have straight shoots. There are two times a year we pick willow sticks. Some people use pine and myrtle to weave with also.

SASHA: How long have you been making baskets?

SHOSH: I learned to weave from my Grandmother when I was 9. When she worked on the eel basket she let me weave with her because she said I had a strong grip. I tried to make my first baby basket when I had my last baby as all the others had one and it was so easy to get babies comfortable in them. But I tried my own design because the one I copied from seemed hard. But when my baby was 5 years old he fell through the bottom so I found that the basket bottoms were designed the way they were for a reason.

Sasha LeMeiux
Grade 2
Hoopa School

* **1993 Art Connects Literary Magazine**. Editors: Atkins, Dr. Amy L., Buckelew, Mary. United States Department of Education Fund for Innovation in Education, 1993.

Today, many California Indians both women and some men, carry on the tradition of basketmaking. Gathering the materials is an important part of making a basket. The materials used for basketry are the same today as they were long ago.

Vivien Hailstone (Karuk-Yurok, member of the Hupa tribe) lives in Redding, California. She works with L.I.F.E. - Local Indians For Education. Vivien speaks to many young people and adults about California Indians today.

Vivien Hailstone is also a basketweaver. Vivien says, "The main thing is, if you are doing basketmaking, you have to have good feelings and good thoughts, and that is why Indians have basket songs. People laugh and enjoy themselves when they are together. If you are feeling sad or if you are angry, you better not even touch the basket, because the basket is part of you."*

*Vivien Hailstone's words are from a special report entitled"California Indian Basketweavers' Gathering, June 28-30, 1991," published in **News From Native California** by Heyday Books, Berkeley, California, Winter, 1991-92, p. 32.

Today basketweavers are faced with many problems when collecting their plant materials. One problem is **pesticides** that are sprayed on the native plants by the United States Forestry Service. Pesticides affect the health of the basketmakers. Pesticides sprayed on the roots and grasses in the fields may be absorbed into the skin and cause illnesses. Another problem is property owners who have fenced the land where native plants grow. Fences keep the Indians from collecting basket materials. Thirdly, logging industries and campgrounds destroy plant gathering areas. Government rules that stop controlled burning of the land are another problem. Basketweavers depend on fire to make the native plants grow stronger. In spite of these problems, the California Indians continue to collect basket materials. At annual meetings of CIBA, the California Indian Basketweavers Association, members discuss these serious problems. The basketweavers are trying to convince the government to stop spraying where native plants grow and allow the Indians to practice land management and controlled burning in their own way. Recently, government agencies have agreed to stop spraying pesticides in certain gathering places in Northern California.[2]

Many people gathered together in the summer of 1993 in Tuolumne, California for the annual meeting of CIBA, the California Indian Basketweavers Association.

Saturday morning all weavers
come together in circles and
circles.
A time for sharing and speaking to·each other.
Joy, tears, hurt. It all is
brought forward.
A Yurok weaver sang basket
songs.
The songs spoke of the shape,
the basket.
In the beginning it sang of a
feeling or something deep
down inside.
Something that you know.
Then the basket, the shape, it
becomes real.
It comes back.
It floats back up the river.
Tears swelled within my eyes
and my heart.
I knew the basket was coming
back.
All of us belonged and we
still do belong.*

—Denise Davis

Denise Davis, a California Maidu Indian, lives in Northern California. Denise is a teacher, artist, and a basketweaver. Denise's artwork and basket weavings are displayed in museums and galleries throughout California.

In winter of 1993, Denise traveled to Europe where she studied art for several months. It was her second trip to Europe where she had demonstrated her basketweaving artistry to many students from all over the world.

* The words of Denise Davis are from a special report entitled "California Indian Basketweavers' Gathering, June 28-30, 1991," published in **News from Native California** by Heyday Books, Berkeley, California, Winter, 1991-92, p. 25.

The California Indians weave beautiful gift baskets. The Pomo gift basket shown here is decorated with mallard duck feathers, meadowlark feathers, clamshell disk beads, and abalone pendants.

TWINED AND COILED BASKETS

There were two main types of woven baskets: twined and coiled. Twined basketry is found among Indian people to the north such as the Shasta, Hupa, Yurok, Tolowa, Modoc, and Northern Wintu tribes.

Close, tight weave twining was used for making household baskets, cooking baskets, and storage baskets. Open weave twining was used for burden baskets, weirs, traps, seedbeaters, winnowers, and baby carriers. Northern tribes that used the twined method of basketry usually did not use any other method.[3]

Coiled basketry is common among Indians in Southern California. Tribes such as the Chumash, Yokuts, Gabrielino, Luiseno, Cahuilla, and Serrano used the coiled method of making baskets. Coiled baskets are woven more closely and take more time to make than twining. A bone awl was used for making openings when weaving coiled baskets. The awl was usually made of part of the leg bone of a deer. The leg bone was split and sharpened to a point. The awl was used to force a space between each coil when adding plant fibers to the basket. Coiling was not used for all baskets. For example, it would be very difficult to make a fish trap in coiled basketry. Southern tribes who used the coiled method, sometimes used the twining method for baskets such as winnowers, trays, seedbeaters, fish traps, or carrying baskets.[4]

Throughout most of California, the women did most of the basketweaving. In tribes such as the Pomo and Wappo, twined fish traps and eel baskets, burden baskets, and basket cradles were made by some of the men.[5] Today, Indian women continue to do most of the basketweaving, but in tribes such as the Pomo, Yuki, and Northern Miwok, some men make twined baskets, cradles, or burden baskets.

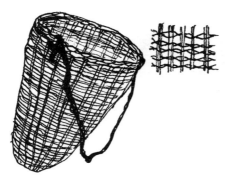

Twined Basket

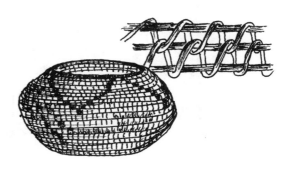

Coiled Basket

BASKET MATERIALS OF THE NORTHERN CALIFORNIA INDIANS

The valleys, meadows, and dry ridges of California were filled with many kinds of coarse, dry grasses, and other natural materials that could be used for making many types of baskets.

Some of the natural materials that the Northern California Indians used to weave baskets were twigs from willow and redbud trees, roots from **conifers**, sedge and bulrush, and shoots from hazel wood. Some coarse baskets were made entirely of willow or tule.

The root of sedge was one of the more important materials the Northern California Indians used for weaving baskets. Sedge roots were cleaned and stripped and put into rolls like twine. The rolls of sedge and other basket-making materials were stored until used.

The Indians used black in many of their basket designs. Sometimes sedge was put into wet ashes to turn it permanently black. Charcoal, iron-rich mud, poison oak, and elderberry juice were also used to dye grasses for black designs. Maiden hair fern stems used by the Hupa, Karuk, and Yurok women gave a glossy black design to many of their beautiful baskets.

Another color commonly used was red. Twigs or branches from redbud and willow trees were gathered and the bark was used for red designs in many baskets. Red color for dyeing basket materials was also made from alder tree bark.[6]

The Achumawi or Pit River Indians made this twined burden basket.

BASKET MATERIALS OF THE SOUTHERN CALIFORNIA INDIANS

The Cahuilla, Luiseno, Tipai,and Ipai and other Indian tribes of Southern California used several materials for basketmaking. Three of the most common materials included a grass called *Epicampes rigens* or Muhlenbergia. This grass was used for the base or foundation of the baskets. Juncus and sumac reeds were used for weaving the basket coils together. *Epicampes rigens,* also called deergrass or bunch grass, was collected, dried, tied into bundles, and stored in the homes of the Indians until it was time for basketmaking. The weaving materials, juncus and sumac, added color to the baskets. The sumac gave a light straw color. It was rarely dyed because it did not dye well. The juncus reed was known for three basic colors: red, natural straw color, and black. Juncus reed has a natural red color that grows on the lowest part of a mature juncus plant at the dirt line. The natural red color is fade proof. Black was made by burying juncus in iron-rich mud for several weeks. Juncus was a popular reed used by the Southern California Indians for basketmaking.

Among all the tribes of California, certain traditions were common to the art of basketmaking. One tradition was that of all the plant materials that were available in California, only certain materials were used for basketmaking. Another tradition in basketmaking was that most tribes specialized in certain types of basketmaking **techniques**. Whether an Indian woman used coiling or twining basketry, the method or technique she learned was usually the technique she used for the rest of her life.[7]

This skillfully woven basket with a rattlesnake design, may be seen at the Malki Museum on the Morongo Indian Reservation in Banning, California.

WATERPROOF BASKETRY

Indian women were able to weave baskets so tightly that the basket was waterproof and could be used for holding mush, stews, and soups. Chumash women living on the Santa Barbara coast and Channel Islands poured melted asphaltum on the inside of some baskets. When the asphaltum was cool, the baskets were waterproof and could hold liquids. Indian women of the southern deserts and mountain areas used pine pitch to line baskets. The Mono and Miwok women sealed the inside of some of their gathering baskets with layers of glue made from the soap root plant.[8]

BOTTOMLESS POUNDING BASKETS

Many California Indian women used bottomless pounding baskets on top of stone mortars when they pounded acorns, seeds, or berries. The bottomless pounding basket was woven and had no bottom. It was attached to the top of the stone mortar with asphaltum. The women used the bottomless pounding basket to keep the acorn meal or pounded seeds from flying out of the mortar.[9]

DECORATED BASKETS

Pomo Indian women wove both twined and coiled baskets. They used a greater variety of designs in their baskets than most other tribes. A Pomo woman's basket design was so **unique** that she could always identify her basket among others by looking carefully at the design. Usually, Pomo women left a break or **dau** in the design to keep away bad luck.

Dating from earliest times, the Pomos were the first people in California to decorate their baskets with feathers. Other tribes used feathers, but rarely covered the entire basket with feathers as the Pomos did. Pomo basketry is still considered among the finest examples of basket art because of their creativity in decorating their baskets with shells, feathers, and combinations of designs.[10]

BOWLS

Some of the Indians who lived in Southern California used clay for making cooking utensils. The Yuma, Mojave, and other Colorado River tribes made clay bowls, cups, jars, and pipes. The Tipai, Ipai, Luiseno, Cupeno, Cahuilla, and Serrano also made clay bowls, jars, and pipes.

Many Indians used the coil method to make pottery. The Indians put finely crushed rock into the clay to make it firmer and stronger. The clay was rolled out into long sausage shapes and coiled on top of a flat clay base. The larger the jar, the more clay coils were used. As each coil was added to the base, the jar was smoothed inside and outside. Smoothing was done by holding a rounded stone on the inside of the jar and gently turning and patting the outside of the jar with a wooden paddle. After drying, the pots were baked in an open wood fire.[11]

The Tubatulabal, the Southern Yokuts, and the Western Mono made another type of pottery. They did not put crushed rock into their clay nor did they use the coil method to make pottery. These tribes put pieces of clay together with a sticky substance to form a bowl or jar. Another way was to mold a bowl or jar out of a lump of clay. All of these ways of using clay for pottery dates back to the earliest times.[12]

Fish Traps Olla. This unique olla (or a storage vessel) was found at Fish Traps in Thermal, California. As yet, the olla has not been dated by experts. Around 1500 A.D., an immense lake covered the desert from Indio, California to Mexico. Indian people from the mountains fished along the shores of ancient Lake Cahuilla. The olla has a stick-like human figure painted on it with rows of hands or paw prints. A similar stick-like human figure is carved in the rocks at Fish Traps. The figure on the olla may be a doctor and the stick next to him is his staff or the Indian doctor in another form. This olla was found near a Bear Doctor's living area. This photo was taken at the Agua Caliente Cultural Museum in Palm Springs.

Chumash Indians in Southern California used a soft, smooth stone called steatite to make bowls, pipes, fish hooks, charms, and beads. The main steatite **quarries** were on Santa Catalina Island. The Chumash traveled to this island by canoe to trade for the steatite. Sometimes they traded with the Island Chumash for large chunks of steatite and other times they traded for bowls already carved from steatite. People of other California tribes were always glad to trade for steatite. Some of these steatite bowls have been found in the Great Central Valley where the Yokuts Indians lived. Steatite eating bowls and water jars were traded as far North as the Chimariko and Shasta tribes. Steatite was one of the many trade items exchanged by the Indians throughout California.[13]

Coastal Indians used abalone shells for bowls and eating utensils. The Chumash Indians made food bowls by plugging the siphon holes of abalone shells with asphaltum. Some times the asphaltum in the holes of the shells was also decorated with tiny inlaid disks of abalone shell.[14]

Some Indians used a soft stone called steatite to make pipes and bowls. This pipe was made in 1993 by Frank Gist, Yurok. It is made of steatite and white oak.

Steatite dishes were traded as far north as the Yurok, Chimariko, and Shasta tribes.

BOATS

The Indians used nature's gifts to build many types of boats. The variety of **watercraft** in California made and used by the Indians was tremendous. Watercraft included **tule** and log rafts, baskets, large clay pots, tule boats, dug-out canoes, and plank boats.

In addition to using boats, the Yuki, Yokuts, and other tribes crossed streams by using large baskets to carry small children, family belongings, or trade goods. The Mojave used large clay pots to carry children or goods across parts of the Colorado River. Swimmers guided the baskets or pots from one side of the river to the other side.[15]

There were three main types of boats used by the native Californians. These were the tule boat, the dug-out canoe, and the plank boat.

Dug-out canoes were of different lengths. Some were as long as twenty feet. You can see the carved seats in this canoe used by the Hupa Indians in 1902.

TULE BOATS

The Indians who lived in areas where tules grew made tule or reed boats. Tules grow in thick clumps near lakes, marshes, creeks, and ponds. The stems of the tules are round and grow from sixteen to eighteen feet in height. Each tule stem is **pithy** and filled with air pockets. The reeds are very light weight so they float easily in the water. Tule boats were made by tying large bundles of dried tules together with twisted tule reeds or strong vines. The tule boat was made high in the front and back and lower on the sides. A man could kneel or stand in the tule boat and pole or paddle himself across lakes or ponds to fish or go through the tules looking for turtles, waterfowl, and eggs. By using tule boats, the Ohlone Indians could paddle to nearby islands to collect bird eggs. Tule boats were also used by Indians along the Carquinez Strait near San Francisco Bay. The tule boat could hold one or more people depending on the size of the boat.

Tule boats were pulled out of the water after each use and allowed to dry so they would not get **soggy** and sink. Even with care, these tule boats were only good for a year.

On September 12, 1984, seven people paddled a tule boat like the ones used by the Indians thousands of years ago, on the waterways from Antioch to Fremont, California. This 78-mile trip took nine days. To make this tule boat, nearly 60 volunteers spent the summer months cutting and bundling more than 5,000 tule stalks. The stalks were lashed into 25-foot-long bundles and roped together with 1,500 feet of tule reeds and braced with willow branches. Paddles were made of oak and willow.

In the deep waters of San Francisco Bay, the Ohlone Indians **navigated** their tule boats with a **double bladed paddle**. A double bladed paddle is a pole with a paddle at either end. Double bladed paddles were not commonly used in California. The double bladed paddle was used mainly by the San Francisco Bay Area Indians for their tule boats. Double paddles were also used by the Chumash. Other Indians such as the Pomo of Clear Lake, navigated their tule boats using a single paddle with a short, broad blade.[16]

DUG-OUT CANOES

A **dug-out** canoe was another type of boat made by the native Californians. The beautiful dug-out canoes of the Yurok and Tolowa Indians were made from fallen redwood trees. Redwood was used because of its size, evenness of grain, and softness. The redwood tree was cut into sections and split. The logs were hollowed out by burning and then the soft **scorched** wood was scraped out with an adze. The Indian craftsmen worked slowly and carefully because a slight mistake could change the whole shape of the boat. It was important to keep the sides and bottom a certain thickness. By tapping and listening to the sides of the canoe, the craftsmen could tell when the proper thickness of the boat was reached. The dug-out canoe was eighteen to twenty-four feet long. It might take a year or two to make the canoe.

The boats were made **watertight** by using pitch or asphaltum to seal out moisture. The Yurok boatbuilders of the North would spread wooden shavings inside the canoe. These shavings were carefully burned and the pitch that oozed from the shavings made the boat watertight. The Yuroks had to be very careful because if the fire got too hot, the boat might crack.

The Yurok redwood dug-out canoes were highly prized as trade items by other Indian tribes. The Yurok canoes were very valuable and were traded for dentalium shells and woodpecker skins and given as marriage gifts. The dug-out canoes were used on the Klamath River, the Trinity River, and other rivers. These canoes were also sturdy enough to be used on the ocean waters along the coast.

Dug-out canoes made from pine, cedar, or fir logs were found in other parts of California and used on rivers, creeks, lakes, and marshes. They were burned, dug out and used for fishing by tribes such as the Nisenan, Shasta, Achumawi, and Chimariko.[17]

PLANK BOATS

Plank boats were made by the Chumash and the Gabrielino Indians of Southern California. In the mountains above their seashore homes these Indians split pine logs into planks by using bone wedges. These planks were carried to the seashore villages where the planks were shaped. The planks were smoothed with rough sharkskin so they would fit together tightly. Starting at the bottom of the boat, each row of planks was put in place with asphaltum. Holes were drilled in the planks with chert tools. The planks were then skillfully fastened together with **thongs** made from deer **sinew** or cord made of milkweed fiber. The thongs or cords were passed through the holes and tied. When the boat was finished, the Indians melted asphaltum, pine pitch, and added red **ochre** color. They smeared the planks with the mixture to make the boat colorful and watertight. Sometimes pieces of abalone shells were used to decorate the outside of the boat.

Plank boats were used in the waters of the Santa Barbara Channel Islands. The boats were twelve to eighteen feet long and could hold as many as twelve men or a great deal of trade goods. The boats were navigated by men using double bladed paddles.

The Chumash, the Gabrielino Indians, and the Channel Island Indians used plank boats.

The Chumash Indians were excellent boatmen. They made frequent trips from their villages on the coast to the villages on the Channel Islands to trade for goods. They also used the boats for fishing in the channel and for hunting seals, sea lions, and sea otters. Sometimes they boated as far south as San Nicolas Island some sixty-five miles away. These wooden boats were very sturdy and were used for many years. Plank boats were often passed on from generation to generation.

The Indians of California respected and cared for their boats. They respected the land that gave them the natural resources to build their boats. They honored their elders for teaching them the skills of boatmaking.[18]

The captains or owners of these seagoing vessels were highly respected by other members of their tribes.

INTERESTING THOUGHTS

Today, only a few Indian people like Axel Lindgren, a Yurok descendant, builds traditional Yurok boats. From redwood logs, Axel carves each beautiful boat eighteen feet long and four feet wide. When the boat is finally finished, it is put in the water. Axel watches carefully. He speaks softly, "You can catch a song by listening to the sound of the water rushing past the bow of the canoe as it cuts through the water. You can. I've done so myself."*

Not too long ago, Linda Gonsalves Yamane, a Rumsien-Ohlone descendant, along with a group of volunteers and park naturalists at Coyote Hills Regional Park in Fremont, built an Ohlone-style tule boat. When the tule boat was finished and ready to launch, Linda remembers, "We eased our twenty-four foot friend into the bay water and the boat was home again. One day it will return completely to the earth, perhaps even nourish a new generation of tules, and the cycle will be complete. Though the ride was not long, it reached back many hundreds of generations for me. I stepped off the boat, but my journey was not complete. There are still many paths to be explored and old ways to relearn. And I will continue to listen as the voices from my past whisper their subtle influences throughout my life."**

* Mr. Axel Lindgren's words are from an article entitled, "The Yurok Redwood Canoe" written by Congor Beasley, Jr., and Guy Mount, published in **News From Native California**, Volume 2, Number 4, Berkeley, California: Heyday Books, September/October, 1988, pp. 18-19.

Linda Gonsalves Yamane's words are from her article entitled, "Ohlone Tule Boat," published in **News From Native California, Volume 2, Number 4, Berkeley, California: Heyday Books, September/October, 1988, p. 16.

BACKTRACKING

Can you answer the following questions?

(1) What problems do California Indians have today when they gather plant materials for basketmaking?

(2) Compare coiled basketmaking to twined basketmaking.

(3) Name five plant materials the Indians used in their basketry.

(4) What two colors in basketmaking were the most common? How did the Indians get these colors?

(5) What natural materials were used by the Indians of Southern California for making bowls?

(6) Name three types of boats used by the California Indians.

(7) What are the advantages and disadvantages of a tule boat?

(8) How was asphaltum used in waterproofing bowls, baskets, and boats?

Linda Yamane, a Rumsien-Ohlone descendant, paddles the tule boat that she helped build.

A Del Norte woman wearing ceremonial regalia

CHAPTER SEVEN
CLOTHING OF THE INDIANS

EVERYDAY WEAR

Throughout most of the year, California weather is warm and sunny. Because of this pleasant climate, the Indians wore very little clothing. Clothing that was worn by the Indians was made from animal skins and plant fibers. The materials used to make clothing depended upon the natural resources available where the Indians lived.

During the warmer months of the year, most Indian men throughout California, wore nothing at all or a **breechcloth** of deerskin. A breechcloth is a piece of deerskin hung, front and back, from a belt-like strip of leather called a thong. The thong circled the man's waist. The thong was an important piece of clothing for a man because, like a belt, he could use it as a holder for a flint or obsidian knife, a rabbit stick, or a skin pouch.

An Indian woman's clothing was a two-piece skirt made of a small front skirt and a larger back skirt. The materials of the skirt varied according to the surroundings and natural resources that were available.

The Yurok maple bark skirt is in one piece. Long ago it was an everyday skirt worn by the women of the tribe.

135

The skirt worn by Indian women of the Karuk, Hupa, Tolowa, Wiyot, Chilula, Eastern Chumash, and other tribes was made of deerskin. Many times the skirts were fringed and decorated with shells, nuts, and seeds. Sometimes, skirts were made of strips of redwood, willow, or maple bark.

The Indian women who lived in Central and Southern California such as the Pomo, Costanoan, Yokuts, Coast Chumash, Luiseno, and others wore skirts made of tule, willow bark, cedar bark, cottonwood bark, and agave fiber. Children under ten years old wore no clothing, but children over ten years followed the clothing habits of their fathers or mothers.[1]

COLDER DAYS

On colder days, the Indians needed more protection. Men, women, and children of Northern California wore deerskin blankets or capes wrapped around their shoulders. The Indians of Central California and Southern California wore capes or blankets made of rabbit fur. Tribes living where there were great numbers of birds such as the Sacramento Valley Area, made blankets of bird feathers. The coverings used for warmth during the cold days were often used as bed coverings at night.

Throughout California, the most popular type of blanket was made with rabbit skins. The Washoe, Mattole, Nongatl, Sinkyone, Lassik, Wailaki, Yokuts, Gabrielino, Tipai, and Ipai as well as many other tribes used rabbit skins to make warm blankets.

The entire rabbit hide was usually cut into one circular piece with an obsidian blade knife. A skillful Indian could cut one hide into a ribbon twelve or fifteen feet long. Several rabbit skins were cut in this manner and tied together to form a chain forty or more feet long. This long fur chain was tied to a tree and twisted into a fur rope and allowed to dry into curled forms. After several of these fur chains had been twisted and allowed to dry, they were woven together with milkweed fibers or Indian hemp into a very warm covering. An adult's blanket required a hundred skins while a child's blanket took about forty skins. Other highly prized skins for blankets were made from sea otters, elk, antelope, California mountain lions, deer, and wildcats.

In some tribes such as the Salinan and Costanoan, the Indians smeared their bodies with mud to help resist the cold.[2]

TANNING HIDES

When the Indians used deerskins for blankets or clothing, they usually **tanned** the hides. The hide was soaked in water or buried in wet ground for several days to loosen the hair on the hide. Then the Indian used a chert scraper or a scraper made of a deer rib or leg bone to remove the hair from the hide. The Indian removed the hair without cutting through the hide. After the hair was removed, the hide was soaked in a special tanning preparation of deer brains and wood ashes or oak gall. The hides were stretched, pulled and kneaded until they were soft and could be made into blankets, breechcloths, skirts, capes, footwear, and dance **regalia**. The softest deerskins were used as baby blankets.[3]

Every member of an Indian family had his own rabbit skin blanket. In the colder parts of California, these blankets could mean the difference between life and death. From infants to the elders, fur or skin blankets were an important part of the Indians' everyday life.

FOOTWEAR

Most of the California Indians did not wear foot coverings except during the cold winter months, on long journeys, hunts, or when gathering wood.

One type of foot covering was ankle-high. It was made from a single piece of buckskin and seamed up the heel and front. This type of low, single-piece footwear was worn by Indians such as the Miwok, Wintu, Hupa, Yurok, Pomo, and Maidu. During cold weather, the footwear was sometimes lined with grass for added warmth. The Modoc, Shasta, Achumawi and others wore footwear with an added sole of elk or bearskin because of the colder climate and rougher ground. The desert Indians, however, when traveling in the mountainous area surrounding their desert home, wore deerskin footwear that reached high up the calf of the leg for protection against brush and rattlesnakes.

The Lassik tribe did not make their footwear like those of their neighbors. The Lassik made their footwear with a single seam going from the little toe to the outer ankle.

Some of the Central and Northwestern tribes used strips of deerskin as drawstrings to hold the footwear on their feet. Each tribe had different ways of tying the drawstrings. Some tribes tied them around the front, back, or side of the ankle. Other tribes such as the Yurok wrapped the drawstrings around the instep of the foot and brought them around to be tied behind the heel.

Indians such as the Pomo, Modoc, and Yokuts living in areas where tules grew made tule sandals. These sandals were worn in place of deerskin footwear. In Southern California Indians also used yucca and agave fiber to make sandals.

Sandals were made of plant fiber and worn by some of the Indians of the Great Central Valley and Southern California.

Snowshoes were made by bending a branch of redbud or willow into the shape of a circle. The two crosspieces were tied with deer sinew.

Indians living along the coast or near the mud flats and marshes used tules to make large round frames for their feet. The Indians could walk in muddy areas without sinking when wearing these tule frames on their feet.

Sometimes, in areas of California where there was snow, the Indians made an oval or kite shaped frame laced with wild grapevine or iris-cord netting. These small hazelwood, redbud, or willow frames were used for moving about in the snow. The hunter would tie his buckskin-wrapped feet onto the snowshoes with deerskin thongs. Modern day snowshoes are fashioned after the snowshoes that the Indians made.[4]

THREAD AND CORD

The women made their own thread and cord for sewing. This thread and cord was made from iris leaves, nettle, agave, yucca, milkweed, or Indian hemp plants. The plants were pounded or rolled until all that was left was strong, string-like fibers.

A woman would take a fiber and roll it up and down her bare thigh and as she added more fibers the cord would grow longer and thicker. When she rolled two pieces of cord together, it made a strong, tightly twisted double cord. Sometimes the cord was light and fine and sometimes it was thick and heavy, but it was always strong.

Cord was used for many things such as sewing clothing and footwear, making rabbit nets, fishnets, carrying nets, and tump lines. Some Indian men of Southern California helped make the thread and cord for their families.[5]

BASKET CAPS

The Karuk, Yurok, Hupa, Chimariko, Shasta, Atsugewi, Maidu, Chumash, Cahuilla and other Indian women wore woven basket caps. These caps were worn by some women every day as part of their dress. These caps were beautifully woven and were not only decorative to the women, but were useful as well.

In some tribes, when a woman went out to gather firewood, plants, roots, or seeds, she wore a tump line over her basket cap to help support a large burden basket on her back. When the burden basket was filled, it was held firmly in place by the tump line that went over the woman's basket cap. In some tribes, such as the Northern Maidu, Karuk, and Salinan, men, women, and children wore basket caps. In other tribes such as the Pomo and Wappo, basket caps were not used.[6]

CEREMONIAL REGALIA

Most of the California Indians had special regalia to wear for ceremonial occasions, such as marking the seasons, coming of age of boys and girls, mourning ceremonies, acorn gathering, deer hunting, and salmon and eel ceremonies. The Indians used many types of decorations for their regalia such as eagle feathers, condor feathers, shells, walrus tusks, pinenuts, and dried juniper berries to make their dance regalia handsome.

Headbands are one of the best known of all California dance regalia. Headbands were made and are still made for wearing in ceremonial feasts and dances. These headbands were made from the feathers of the red-shafted flicker, the red-headed woodpecker, hawks, eagles, yellow hammer, and sometimes the magpie and other birds. Some headbands were decorated with shell beads.

Nancy DiMaggio, Pomo, is wearing a headband made of clamshell disks and beads.

In certain dance ceremonies, some California Indians wore and still wear flicker quill headbands across their foreheads. The headbands are made in the traditional way. The quills for the headbands are scraped with obsidian knives leaving only the dark tufts at the ends of the feathers. These feathers are sewn together to form a long headband. The headband is held in place by a pair of ties at the sides of the head that allow the ends of the headband to flip back and forth as the dancer moves. In days past and sometimes today, Indians combine the headbands with head nets filled with eagle down and feather plumes.

Ralph Moore, Yuki, is wearing dance regalia. His regalia consists of a flicker quill headband, a head net filled with eagle down and a forked feather plume, a netted feather cape, and a deerskin skirt. This photograph was taken in 1900 at Round Valley, Mendocino County, California.

In the White Deerskin Dance, the Hupa Indians wore a wolf tail head-band. Today the Hupa Indians continue the tradition of wearing wolf tail headbands in the White Deerskin Dance. The wolf tail is split lengthwise and the fur covers the forehead and the eyes. The middle part of the head-band is decorated with designs.

The Yokuts made a beautiful dance headdress of magpie feathers with an eagle down crown. The dance skirt was made from strings of milkweed fiber with eagle down twisted into it. Redtail hawk feathers were attached to the base of the skirt.

Cahuilla Indians wore a cap of eagle feathers. The dancer also wore an eagle feather skirt.

A wolf tail headband split lengthwise is decorated with designs and worn so that the fur covers the forehead and eyes.

Susan Burdick, Yurok Indian, is a master basketweaver and teacher. Susan is a member of CIBA, the California Indian Basketweavers Association. Susan makes maple bark skirts, basket caps, and shell-beaded deerskin skirts that are used as dance regalia in traditional ceremonies.

Susan cares for the environment. She is concerned about the pesticides the Forestry Service sprays on native plants used by the Indians for basketweaving. Susan is also concerned about the porcupine. She sometimes uses porcupine quills in her weaving and feels that the porcupine is becoming an endangered species in California. Susan says, "No one is doing any research on protecting the porcupine right now. Porcupines have all but disappeared because the Forest Service poisoned and shot them. Anytime anything is taken from our circle it affects what we do. That little porcupine was put here for a reason — it's not only from our world, it is related to everything else. We need to return the porcupine to our area."

Throughout California, Indians wore strings of clamshell disk beads, dentalium shells, olivella shells, and abalone pendants to add to the beauty of the regalia. The regalia took many hours to make and was highly prized as heirlooms. Today, some of the magnificent regalia remains with the families. Some regalia can be seen in local museums, such as the California Indian Museum in Sacramento.[7]

Today, many California Indians continue to make and use beautiful regalia for traditional dances. Many hours are spent making headbands, dance skirts and capes. Dances are held at special times throughout California to honor the Great Spirit and to thank the Earth for all its gifts.

Cassy Chavez, Hupa, Yurok, and Karuk, is wearing a one-piece everyday maple bark skirt made by her great aunt, Susan Burdick, Yurok. The skirt made of the inner bark of the maple tree is one of three such skirts made by Susan Burdick. There is only one other maple bark skirt made by her people in this century.

TATTOOING

Many Indians of California had their faces or bodies tattooed. Usually tattoos were put on the face rather than on the body. More women were tattooed then men. Among the tribes, tattooing was applied at any age, but it was usual to have the operation done at the age of twelve to fifteen years old. Many Indians could apply the tattooing, but some were considered better at tattooing then others.

The Yurok and Hupa women of high rank tattooed the entire chin from the corners of the mouth downward. Tattooing was done solidly except for two narrow blank lines. This style was common among the women of the Northwestern tribes of California.

The Yuki, Wailaki, and Achumawi women tattooed mostly on the cheeks and did not cover the chin solidly. The Wintu women applied tattoos to the chin in one to three bands running from the lip down. Maidu women made three to seven lines on their chins and also tattooed lines from the corner of the mouth up to the eye. The Northern Yokuts and the Costanoan women tattooed lines or rows of dots on their chins as did other women in Central California who practiced tattooing. In Southern California, Mojave men and women tattooed their chins and foreheads. In other parts of California some tribes practiced no tattooing.

Tattoo marks were made by cutting or pricking a pattern or design on the skin with a very sharp obsidian or flint blade or agave or cactus thorn. When the blood oozed out of the cut or pricked areas, pitch, soot, or charcoal dust was rubbed into the wounds. If a bluish-green color was desired, dye from a certain grass or spider web was used instead of pitch or charcoal. Tattooing was very painful and took a long time to heal.[8]

Yuki

Chimariko

Wailaki

Face tattooing

BODY AND FACE PAINTING

Many Indians of California painted their bodies and faces. Some painted their faces every day. For special ceremonies, body and face painting was used.

The Mojave Indians painted their faces not only for ceremonies, but also to protect their skin against the weather and insects. A Mojave Indian painted his face with a design that he liked and at times, he would create an entirely new design.

Mojave women could not use black face painting, but could apply small amounts of black below their eyes to help stop the glare of the desert sun. White paint was used on the body, but usually not on the face. The Mojave Indians had a custom of saving red or black ground minerals to be sprinkled over their bodies when they died. The shiny mineral used for black was only found in Mojave country and may have been manganese. The red mineral may have been hematite and was received in trade from the Arizona Indians.

The Chumash of the Santa Barbara area used stripes of white paint on their faces and bodies. This white paint was made from **diatomaceous earth**. Body painting was used when celebrating and dancing. When several groups of Chumash gathered for ceremonies each group wore a different pattern so that each could be identified.

The Yokuts and the Shasta people also painted their faces and bodies with paint made from yellow, red, and white minerals and black charcoal. Before the paint was applied to the body, it was mixed with animal grease so that it made a smooth, thick paste. Many Yokuts did not use paint on their faces and bodies every day, but painting was used for special dances or ceremonies.

The Hupa, Yurok, and Karuk used a black face paint during some ceremonies, such as the Jump Dance and Deerskin Dance. The paint is made from the bone marrow of a deer mixed with charcoal from a fire. Many designs are painted on the dancers depending on their part in the dance. Today the Hupa, Yurok, and Karuk still follow the old tradition of face painting for special ceremonies.

Some tribes also made black paint for body and face painting by mixing charcoal with the juice of a baked soap root. White paint was sometimes made from powdered steatite and red paint was made from ground cinnabar. Body paints could be washed away by bathing in a stream or river.[9]

INTERESTING THOUGHTS

Vivien Hailstone is a California Indian. She is Karuk and Yurok as well as a member of the Hupa tribe. She lives in Redding, California and works with a group called L.I.F.E.—Local Indians For Education. Vivien speaks to many young people and adults about the California Indians of the past, but mainly talks about California Indians today.

During a warm summer evening in Davis, California, a large group of young Indian people gathered to hear Elder Vivien Hailstone talk about their Indian heritage. Beautiful new baskets were displayed on a table. The simple lines of very old tobacco baskets shared the same table with the large and small, flat and elegant shapes of Vivien's own personal weaving. Nearby, Vivien's handmade basket medallion necklaces combined old basket making ways with new modern ideas.

To highlight the evening, Vivien brought forth her great-grandmother's two-hundred-year-old deerskin skirts. The young woman who modeled the regalia proudly put on the two-piece deerskin skirts decorated with abalone pendants, strings of tiny clamshell beads, juniper berries, and pinyon nuts. The two skirts were tied around the waist, first the front and then the back. Fringed and decorated, these beautiful skirts were worn with many strands of beads hung around the neck and covering the chest of the young person. As the girl walked about the room, Vivien asked everyone to listen for the song of the skirt. Everyone listened carefully. The soft clink of the shells and beads could be clearly heard as well as the swish of the leather fringe moving to the rhythm of the wearer.

A lovely song of its own. The song of the skirt. The past from great-grandmother. The song of the past is the song of today.

BACKTRACKING

Can you answer the following questions?

(1) What natural materials did Indian men and women use to make their clothing?

(2) What were some of the natural materials used for making string or cord?

How did the Indians make string or cord?

What were some uses for this string or cord?

(3) Why did some Indian women wear basket caps?

(4) What did the Indians use to make their regalia beautiful?

(5) Why do you think some of the Indians had their faces or bodies tattooed?

(6) Why do you think some of the Indians used body or face paint?

(7) Some Indians of the desert used black paint under their eyes to lessen the glare of the sun. Can you think of any people today who might do this?

Costanoan   Maidu

Face Painting

Long ago Yokuts children helped their families gather tule to build a home.

CHAPTER EIGHT
HOMES OF THE INDIANS

The Indians of California used nature's gifts to build many types of homes. Different types of Indian homes were built depending on the climate and natural resources that were available.

PLANK HOMES

In cooler climates of Northern California the Yurok, Hupa, Shasta, Karuk and other tribes built their houses from **slabs** of cedar, pine or fir trees from the mountain forests. The wood for plank houses was obtained by burning down trees or using fallen trees. Indians used deer or elk antlers as wedges to split the tree trunks into planks. The Indians dug a pit and built a plank house over it. On the outside, the walls and roof of the house looked low, but on the inside the dug-out floor allowed room for people to stand. The walls and roof were strong and thick. They made family living cool in the summer and warm in the winter.

Some Hupa plank buildings have stone foundations which date back thousands of years. The building in the front of this picture is the men's sweathouse. The middle building is the main house used for ceremonies and the house in the back is a family house or xonta. The stone area around the xonta was used by the women as a work area and during warm weather the family often ate there.

The inside of a plank house

In the Hupa tribe each family built a **xonta** or plank house. This was their main dwelling where the family ate and the women and children slept. In their xonta each family kept their tools and personal belongings. The xonta could be as large as twenty feet square and was partly built underground. In the middle of the xonta was a sunken living area which was reached by a plank ladder. The main living area was four to five feet beneath ground level and this area was lined with planks like the outside of the house. A fire could be built in the sunken center area of this two-level home for warmth and cooking.

As the Indians entered the doorway of the xonta there was a storage space above the sunken living area. In this area the Indians stored baskets of dried fish, meat and seeds, wood for the fire, and necessary tools.

Near the fire, in the center of the house, the family gathered together. Indian men and special visitors sat farthest from the door, away from any cold drafts that might enter through the doorway. Next to the men sat the women and children. Less important members of the group sat nearest the doorway.

The Hupa men slept in the **sweathouse** or **taikyuw**, also made of planks. It was built similar to a plank house, but it did not have storage areas. The men took sweat baths in the taikyuw. In the afternoons the men lit a fire in the firepit of the taikyuw for a sweat bath. They sat around the fire leaning against carved wooden headrests. When a man finished his sweat bath he dashed to a nearby stream to bathe in the cool waters. Later, he relaxed in the sun, ate with his family, and then returned to the taikyuw to smoke, talk, pray, and sleep.[1]

The redwood plank home of the Yurok people was more than just a shelter. To the Yuroks the redwood was a spirit and the house planks actually lived and breathed. The Yuroks gave their homes a name and the family was known by that name. Modern Yuroks have built a village near Patrick's Point, California to show how the Yuroks lived long ago. The homes were built using their people's ancient ways. The planks of the houses were split from redwood logs with elkhorn antler wedges and the poles lashed together with vines.

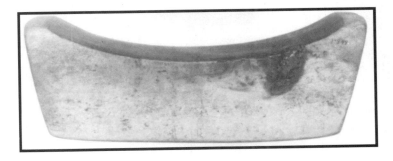

Wooden headrests were used by the Indian men in the sweathouse.

BARK HOMES

The mountain tribes such as the Wintu, the Mono, and Maidu lived in bark dwellings. Bark dwellings were built by coastal and mountain Indians who could obtain thick slabs of bark from nearby redwood and cedar trees by using elk-horn wedges. These slabs of bark were sometimes piled against a central pole until all holes were covered except a smoke hole in the top and a small doorway down below. Often during cold weather a door of tule or animal skin was used. A bark dwelling could house a family of six, but during the summer months the Indians lived outside and used their winter dwelling as a storehouse.[2]

Miwok bark homes at Chaw-se Grinding Rock Park, in Pine Grove, California

Indians that lived where the tules grew made thick walled homes with bundles of tule stalks. This large tule home was built by rangers and volunteers and can be seen at Coyote Hills Regional Park in Fremont, California.

BRUSH HOMES

You have learned that Indians of the far north, such as the Yurok, Tolowa, Hupa and Karuk tribes, built their homes of planks. You have also learned about the bark houses of the mountain tribes. Indian homes differed depending on geography, climate, and materials available.

In the valley, along the coasts, and in the southern desert areas, most homes were built using tules or brush. The Valley Pomo, Wappo, Plains Miwok, Yokuts, Chumash, and other tribes built homes of brush or tule. The brush house was round or **oblong** in shape, some were small and some were large. Generally the floor was dug about two feet deep. Sometimes the floor was round and sometimes it was oblong. The Indians used digging sticks, and sharp stones and shells to loosen the soil. Baskets were used to remove the soil from the floor. This dug-out floor provided a smooth area for the home and prevented floor drafts. Next, a frame of willow poles was made to curve over the floor. The frame was then covered with brush or

The size of each Desert Cahuilla brush home or Kish depended on the size of the family. The house was built with a firepit in the center of the room and a smoke hole in the roof. The floor of the home was dug out a few inches. The floor hardened with daily use. Mesquite or creosote frames were covered with arrowweed, palm fronds, or desert willow. The brush was lashed together with yucca fiber rope. A shaded ramada at the end of the house provided a cool area on hot desert days.

tules that were tied with cord made from nettle, milkweed, or Indian hemp fiber. A small opening at the top of the brush home allowed smoke to escape. If a large brush **communal** home was planned, an oblong floor was dug and poles were placed in two rows down the long sides of the home to support the long roof. Several families could live in these houses.

The Yokuts people, living in the Great Central Valley, were one of the largest Indian groups in California. They built as many as five kinds of brush dwellings. The home most commonly used was the brush house that was built over a two-foot deep pit. When the Spanish expeditions of Fages and Crespi (1772) and Anza and Font (1776) came through the Great Central Valley, they saw many types of brush shelters skillfully built by the Indians. Fortunately, these explorers kept written diaries of what they saw so today we have an accurate description of Indian homes.

One of the most interesting brush houses built by the California Indians was the Yokuts' tule mat-covered communal house. As many as five or six families or a small village could live in a home of this kind. In these large dwellings, the Yokuts as in all Indian tribes, were aware of each family's privacy. Each family had its own living area, firepit, and private entrance. These communal dwellings could have been as long as three hundred feet and had a door at each end.

Another type of brush home built by some tribes was used only by women or teen-aged girls. This home was built over a frame and covered with tules and brush much like a brush house. Its size depended on the number of women living in the village and was used by women on special occasions. Tribes in Northern California used wood to build these special homes for women.

In summer, the Indians often built **temporary lean-tos** or flat-topped brush shelters made mainly to keep out the sun. These shelters were used by most Indians in their villages and were also excellent as temporary homes when some tribes moved into the cooler hills during the warmer months.[3]

EARTH-COVERED BRUSH HOMES

Throughout California, various tribes of Indians such as the North-Central Yana, Yuki, Plains Miwok, Yokuts, Luiseno, Cahuilla, Tipai, and Ipai used an earth covering on their brush homes. These earth-covered homes were dug down deeper than the floor of a regular brush home. This dug-out floor helped keep out summer's heat and winter's cold.[4]

SWEATHOUSES

Most Indians throughout California built sweathouses. The Indians of Northern California built their sweathouses of wooden planks.

Tribes such as the Miwok and Ohlone built sweathouses of brush or brush covered with mud. These sweathouses were built near a river or stream and usually had a dug-out floor. The walls of the sweathouse were often covered with a thick layer of mud and the entrance was made small so that a tribal member had to bend over in order to enter. Small entrances kept the heat from escaping and the sweathouse stayed warm throughout the night.

The sweathouse of the Yokuts of the Great Central Valley was oblong and its floor was dug out two or three feet deep. Thick poles were used as a sturdy framework to support a heavy roof made of brush, tules, and mud. The roof was low and the entrance was small. As with most Indian tribes, the Yokuts' sweathouse was never more than a short distance from the water and was usually located downstream from the village.

Some Cahuilla Indians of Southern California built their sweathouse above ground without a dug-out floor. Four poles were set in the ground about ten feet apart. Another pole was used to bridge the four poles. The cross pole became the main beam in the sweathouse roof and other poles were leaned against it from all sides to form a tent-shaped structure. Brush and mud were packed on the sides and a low opening was left for a door.

Throughout California, sweathouses were commonly used by the men. In a few tribes, however, women were allowed to enter. Maidu women of the North and the Tubatulabal of the South would take their children to the sweathouse. Some Indians such as the Pomo allowed women in their sweathouses at certain times and for special occasions, receiving a cure, singing, or just observing. Women doctors could come into the sweathouse at anytime.

Once or twice daily, the men gathered in the sweathouse. A fire of red hot stones was used to make the Indians sweat heavily. As the house got hotter and hotter, the men began to sweat. They used an animal bone to scrape the sweat from their bodies. When the sweat was running off their bodies, they would run outside and jump into a nearby stream.

Some Indians used the sweathouse for games and **initiation** ceremonies. A sweathouse could also be used as a place for curing an illness. Sometimes herbs were added to the fire so the fumes would make a pleasant odor and help with the cure. The Miwok tribes, like many other tribes, used the sweathouse for purification before going deer hunting.

The North Fork Mono sweathouse was earth-covered. It was a gathering place for men. The men took sweat baths in the late afternoon and then took a quick dip in a nearby stream. Women and girls stayed away from the sweathouse, but boys sometimes were allowed to stay close by and listen to stories told by the elders.

The Mojave people did not have sweathouses. Instead, sometimes important men asked friends and family to help build a large home. This home had a frame of logs and poles and was thatched with brush. It was then covered with sand. This house was large and many people could sleep there. Each family or single person had certain sleeping areas inside this one large room. Late in the afternoon, a fire was built just inside the door of the house. At night, the fire was covered with sand and the heat from the fire as well as the warmth of the sleeping families kept away the chill of the cold desert nights.[5]

Today at Patrick's Point in Northern California, Yuroks have built a replica of a village called Sumig. The Yurok sweathouse looks as it would have looked hundreds of years ago.

CEREMONIAL OR DANCE HOUSES

Most Indian tribes throughout California had a village **ceremonial** house that was sometimes called a round house or dance house. This house was the center of many ceremonies and social gatherings.

Some Pomo Indians built large ceremonial houses which were circular in shape. A floor was dug out five to six feet deep with fire-hardened sticks and the dirt was carried off to one side to be used later in finishing the roof. The dug-out floor was about fifty feet wide and five large posts supported the roof timbers which rose to eighteen feet in height. The roof timbers were covered with brush and the dirt which had been dug out was brought back and packed down on the roof. As many as seven hundred Indians could gather here.

The Yuki Indians built their ceremonial houses with a dug-out floor and a dome-shaped roof. These houses were covered with brush and then packed with earth. The Yuki earth-covered ceremonial houses could hold one hundred to two hundred or more Indians.

Cahuilla Indians used a large ceremonial house known as a **kishumnawat.** This house was used for ceremonies, curing, and recreational activities. The kishumnawat was usually circular with a sunken floor. The roof slanted upward from the walls and was supported by forked posts. Willow, arrowweed, and palm fronds were used to make the roof.

The ceremonial houses of the Sierra Miwoks were dug into the ground about three to four feet deep and measured fifty to sixty feet from side to side. The dug-out sides were **reinforced** with large rocks so that the sides of the dance house would not collapse. Inside the dance house and standing about twenty-five feet apart were four huge tree trunks sunk a few feet into the earth dancing floor. The four huge trunks had natural forks or **clefts** at the top of each trunk and these four trunks supported four large logs that were arranged in a square shape. This square shape supported poles which rose to a height of twenty feet from the earth floor.[6]

Salvador, a member of the Wintu tribe, is dancing around the pole in front of the round house at Cortina Valley in Colusa County, May 1906.

This Miwok round house at Chaw-se Grinding Rock Park in Pine Grove, California was built about twenty years ago. It is a sacred building and people are not allowed to take pictures inside. The Indians have sacred ceremonies in this round house with prayers, singing, and dancing.

Bill Franklin, the man on the next page, is a Miwok Indian and helped build three round houses in Northern California including this one at Chaw-se Grinding Rock Park. Bill Franklin learned to do traditional Miwok dances when he was twelve years old. He learned to dance by watching the other dancers. He knew that his goal was to dance with the elders. He wanted to be like the elders and later when he became a dancer, he thought that dancing was one of the greatest things he could ever do.

Bill Franklin, Miwok, grew up in Ione, but now lives in Sloughhouse, California with his grandson, Don. Bill has been working to preserve his Miwok Indian culture for more than forty years. He has helped in the Indian Education Program in the Elk Grove School District. Bill is the founder of the California Indian Dance and Cultural Group, now called the Miwok Dance Group. He is a member of the Native American Heritage Commission and is an honored elder in the California State Indian Museum in Sacramento.

Today as Bill continues to work with the fifteen-member Miwok Dance Group, his encouragement to all young California Indian people is to keep their traditions alive and continue the Indian culture by learning the dances and songs and helping to teach them to others.

INTERESTING THOUGHTS

Brandon Biondini, Tashina Andreoli, and Christina Kinder wrote these stories when they were in Mrs. Jennifer George's fifth grade at the Hoopa Elementary School in Northern California. Their stories were published in the **1993 Art Connects Literary Magazine**.

---

*HOOPA

Hoopa is a nice little town in Northern California, on the Hoopa Valley Indian Reservation. Our area has lots of salmon, and some deer, and there is a river running through the valley.

There are a lot of beautiful mountains here, and the air is fresh and the water is clean. We log timber and there are a lot of Indians and some white people, and we have a lot of creeks.

Brandon Biondini

* * * * *

*HOOPA

Hoopa is a little town along the Trinity River. There's about 2000 people in Hoopa. There are 2 stores, 1 small and 1 big store. There is also 1 bank, and 2 gas stations, 2 restaurants and 1 motel. Hoopa is 12 miles square. Hoopa is very small compared to a city. Hoopa is open country. I love Hoopa because I like open country. I like the river that runs through Hoopa.

Tashina Andreoli

* * . * * *

*HOOPA VALLEY

In my home at Hoopa Valley, I have fun with my three brothers and my dog. At school, I play with my friends and when the bell rings, it is time to go for a walk.

After school my brothers and I do our homework. When we're finished, we fix a snack and go out to play.

In the evening, my family watches the "Discovery Channel" then my grandmother and I make dinner. Then we have a dessert and watch more T.V. a little, and then we all go to bed.

Christina Kinder

---

*1993 Art Connects Literary Magazine. Editors: Atkins, Dr. Amy L., Bucklew, Mary. United States Department of Education Fund for Innovation in Education, 1993.

BACKTRACKING

Can you answer these questions?
(1) Name four kinds of houses the California Indians built.

(2) Tell how a plank house and a brush house were alike. Tell how a plank house and a brush house were different.

(3) What materials did the Indians use for tools to build their homes?

(4) Look at your California Indian map and locate five tribes living in different areas of California. Tell what natural resources they would have used to build their homes.

(5) Some tribes put an earth covering over their brush homes. The floor was dug down deeper than regular brush homes. Why?

(6) How was the sweathouse used by Indian men and women?

By dancing with his elders, this young Indian boy is learning some of the traditions of his people.

CHAPTER NINE
CUSTOMS AND CEREMONIES

BELIEFS AND CUSTOMS

The Indians' lives centered around their religious beliefs. These beliefs were the basis for their own tribal customs. They followed strict religious and social rules. These rules served as a guide in the daily lives of the Indians. There was cooperation among families and early in life each child learned to follow the ways of his tribe. Often grandparents, aunts, uncles, and cousins lived with the family. All the relatives were part of a large group called an **extended family**. Each person had a responsibility to one another. Grandparents and older members of the family helped take care of the smaller children. By listening to the elders, the child learned the history and traditions of his people. By observing parents and older brothers and sisters at work, the child learned sharing, patience, and skills. As the child grew older and took on responsibilities of his own, he used the skills and values he had learned from his family to guide him as a responsible person in his tribe.

Indian daily life was based on a religious belief that honored the spirits of animals, trees, and rocks. The Indians believed that the Great Spirit was more powerful than all of the other spirits.

Throughout most of California, many Indians honored the Coyote or Eagle as creators of the world. They believed the Great Spirit often took the form of Coyote and Eagle to create the world. Many tribes believed that Eagle and Coyote were also the creators of the Indians.

Eagle was important to some Indian groups because he was said to live forever and was a symbol of life after death. Eagle was respected by the Indians and eagle feathers were used only in special ceremonies.

Coyote was a **cunning**, clever animal and was perhaps more like a person because of his human qualities. Coyote was known for his humor, kindness, generosity, and patience. He was also known to be selfish and boastful and a trickster. Coyote taught the Indians the correct way to live. The Indians respected all animals because each animal was a part of the creation stories that were told over and over again.

The Indians accepted good and bad spirits. They felt that the good spirits were always near and brought good luck. Whenever a tribe had trouble such as sickness, floods, earthquakes, fires, accidents, and lack of food, the tribe believed that the balance and harmony with nature had been disturbed. The leader of the tribe called for special ceremonies that included prayer, singing, and dancing. These ceremonies restored balance and harmony with nature.[1]

INDIAN LEADERSHIP

All tribes in California had leaders or headmen or headwomen. There were certain people in the tribes who were leaders because of their influence, wealth, responsibility, and intelligence. Leadership was usually **inherited** and most of the time the leader was wealthy. Often a leader was assisted by a council of men or women who gave advice. The leader's council was usually made up of people over forty years old, elders, who often were close relatives of the leader. Before a person became a leader, he usually had served as an advisor on the council of elders.

The leader set the time for ceremonies and helped to solve daily problems. The leader gave advice to the people and watched over the conduct of his people.[2]

The Modoc, the Achumawi, the Shasta, the Mountain Miwok, and the Wintu leaders appointed a leader to lead their men in invasions of neighboring tribal areas. Disagreements might start because of dishonest trading, paying no attention to boundaries, stealing, or kidnapping. The tribal leaders were responsible for making peace between the tribes. Sometimes dentalium shells, baskets, deerskins, foods, or other goods were used to pay back losses.[3]

When necessary, the Karuk Indians wore fighting armor. This picture was taken in 1907.

Leaders of the Hupa, Yurok, and Karuk tribes of Northern California were called upon to settle arguments within the tribe. They talked with neighboring tribal leaders about problems such as fishing rights or trading. The way disputes were settled between the Hupa, Yurok, and Karuk tribes was very different from other California Indians. A settlement dance was held. The men who were taking part in the dance stood in a row. The men's faces were painted black and they were fully armed with their weapons. Many yards away stood their enemies. Before the settlement dance took place, the money or property to be paid back by each side was put in baskets by the fire. The baskets of money and property were sung over. After this came the settlement dance with each tribe moving side by side. Finally the payments were made to each side and the dispute was settled.[4]

The many Yokuts tribes of the Great Central Valley had a leader for every village. In larger villages there were assistant leaders who were responsible to the head leader. All Yokuts had a special helper or **winatun** whose duty was to greet all travelers, discuss their business and if necessary, take them to the leader. Having a winatun was a custom that allowed the leader time for other important duties. Although there may have been as many as 20,000 Yokuts or more living in the Great Central Valley, tribal leaders respected each other's rights and property, thus, the leaders had few major problems.[5]

The tribes of Southern California had leaders who inherited their positions. When a leader died, he passed the position on to a son, a brother, or a cousin. If a leader had two sons, he had the right to select the son he felt would do the best job. Southern tribes such as the Serrano, Luiseno, Cahuilla, Ipai, Tipai, and Gabrielino were friendly and were linked by trading and sometimes by marriages. Because of these connections, there was very little hostility among the tribes.[6]

The Mojave tribes in the Southeastern section of California had tribal leaders and some tribes had two or three assistant leaders. The Mojave were friendly with neighboring tribes such as the Tipai, Chemehuevi and Cahuilla, but they had many wars with the Halchidhoma tribe of the Colorado River area. The Mojave also fought with Arizona tribes.[7]

Throughout California, all leaders had to prove themselves as good leaders. Leaders were dignified, had courage, were calm under pressure, and had wisdom when working with people.

The duties of the leader were to see that food was shared equally among the people, to bring peace between quarreling families or villages, and to organize trading expeditions. The leader also welcomed traders to the village, helped direct ceremonies, and encouraged the people to lead cooperative and productive lives.[8]

Sergeant Sambo was born in 1865 at a rancheria near the Klamath River. His grandfather, Maw-Qwa-Haw-O, was the leader of four Shasta tribes, the Shasta Valley tribes, the Quartz Valley tribe, the tribe along the Klamath River to the mouth of the Scott River, and the tribes around Jacksonville in Oregon. These tribes spoke the same language known as the Kik-ut-sik language. Sergeant Sambo's father became the leader of two of the Shasta tribes. When Sergeant Sambo was born, his father named him Sergeant after an officer at Fort Jones. Sergeant was the last of his people who could speak the Kik-ut-sik language. He died in 1963, almost 100 years old.

INDIAN DOCTORS

Throughout California there were several types of Indian Doctors. Sometimes Indian Doctors became almost as important as the leader or headman of the tribe.

One type of doctor was the Herb Doctor. He or she sang and danced and used roots, herbs, and native plants to help cure sick people. The Herb Doctor collected and carried these herbs in pouches or baskets. The Herb Doctor cured such illnesses as eye infections, stomach pains, coughs, and toothaches.

Another type of doctor was the Healing Doctor. He or she had special powers and received these powers from dreams and spirits that entered the body. Often the Healing Doctor inherited his position from a relative and trained with an experienced doctor before he or she could treat patients. This doctor's healing powers would cause bad spirits to leave the body of a sick person. The Healing Doctor **diagnosed** what was believed to be causing the sickness in a patient and sometimes sucked the affected part of the patient's body to remove the poison. When this Healing Doctor cured someone, the spirit within the doctor's body did the healing. This type of doctor was called upon when a person became very ill. The Healing Doctor sang, danced, and used his or her own special powers to cure the person. The songs the doctor used remained his or her own personal songs and the doctor did not have to share them with other doctors.

If the Healing Doctor could not cure a patient, the members of the tribe might try to put the doctor to death. The people gave the doctor money or gifts to help cure ill friends and relatives. If a person died, the doctor had to give back the gifts. If the sick person got well, the doctor became more important.[9]

OTHER TYPES OF DOCTORS

There were other types of doctors such as the Rain or Weather Doctor, the Rattlesnake Doctor, and the Bear Doctor.

The Rain Doctor had control over the weather. He would conduct special ceremonies to bring rain or stop flooding. There were more Rain Doctors in the lower Central Valley and in the Southern part of the state than in Northern areas.[10]

Sinel was a Tache Yokuts Rain Dancer and Doctor. He is wearing ceremonial regalia that he made. He used eagle down to make his skirt, sparrow hawk feathers for ear ornaments, and raven feathers and red-tailed hawk or eagle down for his headdress. Sinel was known for his special healing powers.

The Rattlesnake Doctor was known in various parts of California. This doctor cured or prevented snake bites. Yokuts doctors had elaborate ceremonies that included the juggling of live rattlesnakes. The Yokuts would not kill a rattlesnake because they believed that the rattlesnake could cause a person to die without striking him. Rattlesnake dances were held throughout the Great Central Valley.[11]

The Bear Doctor was found in most all Indian villages. He had the power to turn himself into a grizzly bear so that he could destroy the enemies of the tribe. The Bear Doctor received his power from the very strong and **ferocious** grizzly bear. A Bear Doctor was often feared by tribe members, but he was a necessary member of the tribe because he could destroy enemies. The Yokuts of the Great Central Valley and the Cahuilla Indians of Southern California had stories telling that the Bear Doctor could actually turn himself into a grizzly bear. The Wintu, Pomo, Yuki and other tribes believed the Bear Doctor had special powers, but that he only dressed in bearskins and was not actually transformed into a bear.

The Rain Doctor and Rattlesnake Doctor were better known in the Southern part of the state. The Bear Doctor was known throughout the entire state from the Shasta Indians in Northern California to the Ipai and Tipai Indians in Southern California.[12]

L. Styles

*THE RATTLESNAKE AND TO

Every morning, Man-el, the moon maiden, took Mukat's people and animals to the water, and they would spend the day there, swimming and playing happily together and learning the wonderful songs that Man-el taught them. The people were always ready to laugh, too, at one of their number, a tiny man called To, who was most amusing when he danced or sang a song.

There was one animal that always stayed behind with Mukat when Man-el and the others went to the water. This was Rattlesnake, who remained coiled up beside Mukat's door. In those days Rattlesnake had neither teeth or poison.

Every evening when the people and the animals returned to Mukat's big house, To jumped on top of the Rattlesnake's head and danced and sang. Although To was very tiny his constant dancing made Rattlesnake's head flatter and flatter. Finally Rattlesnake complained to Mukat. Mukat promptly pulled out two short whiskers to which he added poison before giving them to Rattlesnake for teeth.

"Now," said Mukat to Rattlesnake, "when To comes back and starts to dance upon your head you can bite him. But once you have bitten him you must leave my big house and hide among the rocks."

The next time tiny To danced upon Rattlesnake's head the reptile bit him and then followed Mukat's warning and hid among the rocks. Rattlesnake was the first animal to leave Mukat's house, and he never returned to it.

* This story about a rattlesnake is a small part of the Creation story called "Man-el, The Moon Maiden," told by Harry C. James, Cahuilla, in his book, **The Cahuilla Indians**. Published herein courtesy of Malki Museum Press.

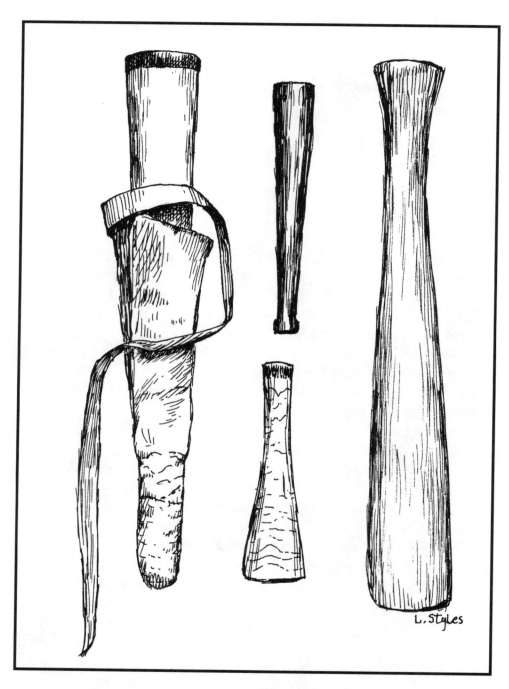

Ceremonial pipes of California Northwestern Indians

TOBACCO

Tobacco was an important part of religious ceremonies. In many tribes, Indian doctors smoked tobacco before ceremonies. They blew the smoke in the sacred directions—north, east, west, south, and up. This helped to clear the ceremonial area of any bad forces.

In some tribes tobacco was an important part of the men's Deer Hunting Ceremony. Several days before the hunt, the men went to the sweathouse. There tobacco was smoked and sometimes eaten with shell lime as part of the men's purification before deer hunting.

One of the earliest uses for tobacco leaves was for medicine. Tobacco leaves were applied to the head to relieve headaches. Seeds of these plants were used to ease toothaches. Juice from the tobacco plant was put on cuts and sores. To help cure an earache, smoke was blown into the ear and then a warm pad was placed over the ear.

There were several types of tobacco plants native to California. Most tobacco was obtained from plants that grew wild, but seeds were sometimes planted by the Hupa and Yurok. The **cultivated** plants produced big leaves and had better flavor. The Indians gathered the whole plant when the seeds were ripe, but the leaves were green.

The Tubatulabal women stripped tobacco leaves from the wild plants, sun-dried the leaves, sprinkled them with water, and dried them again. After several days, the leaves were pounded into a fine powder, mixed with water, formed into balls, and stored. The Tubatulabal, as well as the Kitanemuk, Yokuts, and Chumash sometimes mixed tobacco with shell lime and ate it.

Tobacco was smoked in tubular pipes. Northern California Indians used hardwood pipes with a steatite inset. Southern California Indians used stone or clay pipes. The Indians of the Great Central Valley and further south used cane to make pipes. Indians living along the coast used elderberry pipes. Mountain Miwok Indians smoked tobacco in tubular pipes made of oak, ash, maple root, manzanita, or elderwood.

Although tobacco was used by both Indian men and women, it was used mostly for religious ceremonies and special celebrations.[13]

The use of tobacco today is different from the way tobacco was used in the past. When the Indians used tobacco in religious ceremonies it was for special purposes and not used daily.

DEATH

Throughout California the Indians had many customs about death. Death was held in high respect by all the Indians and they showed their concern for the **deceased** person in many special ways.

Many tribes **cremated** the deceased. Many tribes like the Wiyot, Mattole, Nongatl, Sinkyone, and others buried the deceased in cemeteries located not too far from the village. Some tribes such as the Wintu and Karuk buried the deceased close to their own homes in family-owned grave plots.[14]

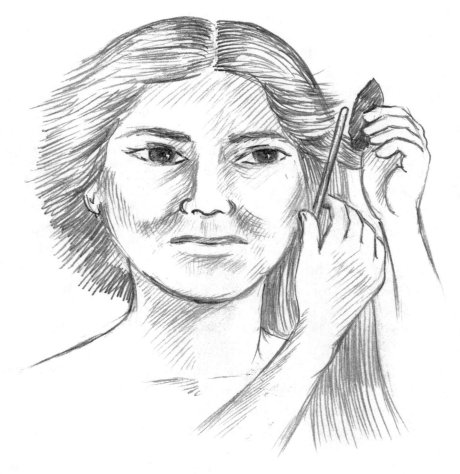

A mourning custom of some Indians was to burn off their hair. When the hair was burned, it was tightly held between split sticks and singed off with burning bark.

In most of California personal belongings were burned or put in the grave with the deceased. Clothing, bows, arrows, knives, and baskets were some of the personal belongings. Sometimes these valuables were broken and sometimes left unbroken. In the Wintu tribe there was always a bowl of acorn meal water put beside the grave for the soul to drink. The Hupa people hung the clothing of the deceased person on the limbs of bushes and trees in the forest.[15]

In some tribes such as the Hupa, Chilula, Whilkut, Yana, and Wintu, men and women relatives showed their love and respect for the deceased by cutting or singeing off their hair close to the head. Pitch was sometimes rubbed in the hair and the face was covered with charcoal, pitch, and powdered clamshells.[16]

After a few days, the soul of the deceased journeyed to the sky or Western Mountains.[17] In some tribes no mention was made of the deceased person's name. The deceased person's name was never mentioned again because the deceased must continue his or her journey alone to the sky and not return for a companion. Respect for the dead was further shown when many years after the death of a loved one, a child was named after this person.[18]

CEREMONIES

Indians throughout California had many types of ceremonies. Usually the religious leader of the tribe set the time for the ceremonies and the Indian Doctor led the ceremonies. These ceremonies included singing and dancing and praying and often lasted many days. Each ceremony had a special purpose and was passed down from generation to generation. These ceremonies were explained through stories handed down through **oral tradition** by the elders of the tribe. Children watched these ceremonies and sometimes took part in them. As the children grew up, these ceremonies given to the Indians by the Great Spirit became a very important part of their lives.[19]

MOURNING CEREMONY

The Mourning Ceremony was held by nearly all Indian tribes in California such as the Konkow, the Yokuts of the Great Central Valley, the Monache, and the tribes of the South, such as the Gabrielino, Ipai, and Tipai. This ceremony was held one year after the death and funeral of a person. The Mourning Ceremony was held for all the people of the tribe who had died during the year. The relatives of the deceased worked very hard during the months before the Mourning Ceremony making baskets and gathering food. Friends and relatives from nearby tribes were invited and asked to help with the ceremony. The ceremony usually lasted a week. Life-size **images** of each deceased person were made of tule or cattails. These images were clothed and containers of food and water were placed in a carrying net on the back of each image for the long journey into the lands of the Great Spirit. Singing, dancing, crying, praying, storytelling, and **feasting** took place and finally the tule images were burned along with the last gifts and possessions of the deceased. This burning released the souls of the deceased into the spirit world.

The tribes of the North, such as the Yuki, Pomo, Hupa, and others had a funeral immediately following the death of a person, but did not have a Mourning Ceremony a year later. Instead, these tribes remembered the deceased at major ceremonies throughout the year. Perhaps, during a dance ceremony, an older person would remember a friend or relative and begin weeping. Others would join in the weeping as they, too, remembered former relatives and friends who had taken part in the ceremony with them. The Hupa and the Yurok had a special place in their dance area reserved for the spirits of those who had gone on. Living persons were not allowed in that area. Thus, a part of some ceremonies became a time for remembering the deceased.[20]

The Ipai, Tipai, and other tribes in Southern California made deer-toe rattles. The rattles were used only one time and then burned in the mourning ceremony. Each rattle used the feet of four or five deer. The deer feet were boiled in water for several hours and then the toes were knocked off and cleaned out with bone tools. Holes were made in the tips of the toes and agave fiber was used to string and knot each toe on a six- inch cord. These rattles made a pleasing sound.

INITIATION CEREMONIES

Two other very important ceremonies that took place in tribes throughout California were the Boys' and Girls' **Initiation** Ceremonies. These ceremonies marked the passage of boys and girls from childhood to adulthood and usually took place when the young people were about twelve or thirteen years old. In these ceremonies the young people were taught the ways of the tribe and given advice like the following words from the Luiseno—"Have respect for elders, keep from anger, be polite to family members." Doing these things was a guarantee that they would grow old in good health, have children who honored them, and when they died their spirits would go to the sky. [21]

BOYS' INITIATION CEREMONY

During the Boys' Initiation Ceremony an older man was appointed as advisor or protector to one young man. This advisor would be available to advise the boy the rest of his life. Sometimes, another tribal family was asked to help with the Boys' Initiation Ceremonies. In some tribes, Jimson Weed or Angelica was pounded and used in a tea and each boy drank a little of the tea under the watchful eye of his advisor. This tea gave the boys dreams that told of their future lives. During the ceremony, the boys were told the secrets of the universe and the traditions and history of the tribe. Often they were given tests of bravery and courage before their final initiation as an adult member of the tribe.[22]

GIRLS' INITIATION CEREMONY

Many Indian tribes throughout California celebrated a growing-up time in young girls' lives. The Girls' Initiation Ceremony was a great event and a time for feasting, singing, dancing, and games. The initiation ceremony was attended by friends and relatives and gifts were given. The girls were advised by older women just as the boys had been given advice by older men. The girls were told about the duties of womanhood and special secrets of the universe. Both the Boys' and Girls' Initiation Ceremonies meant that these young people were ready to take their places as young adults in the tribe.[23]

OTHER CEREMONIES

There were many other tribal ceremonies throughout California. Religious ceremonies of some of the Northern California tribes included the White Deerskin Dance, the Boat Dance, the Jump Dance, and the Brush Dance as well as Eel and Salmon Ceremonies. Religious ceremonies of Southern California tribes included Owl and Deer Dances, Eagle Dances, and Bird Dances. Many tribes had ceremonies including Spring Ceremonies, Bear and Rattlesnake Ceremonies, Marriage, Birth, and Child-Naming Ceremonies, Acorn Ceremonies or Agave Ceremonies as well as other ceremonies. Most of the Indian ceremonies were religious ceremonies. When the Indians danced and sang and prayed, they were keeping a promise made to the Great Spirit.

The White Deerskin Dance is celebrated every other year in Northern California on the Hoopa Indian Reservation. This picture was taken in the year 1903.

INTERESTING THOUGHTS

The last rays of the setting sun shine through a forest near a wide river. It is late summer and the sun flashes long golden rays off the waters as the river quietly flows past many Indian homes. The air is warm and all is still. Then, like thunder in the far distance, the foot drums signal the beginning of a ceremony. Gradually the music becomes louder. Rattles, whistles, and the sound of voices can be heard. Soon dancers appear wearing dance regalia. The feather headdresses bow and sway ever so gently as the Indian dancers bend forward and backward. Evening darkens the land. The blaze of the fire **silhouettes** the figures of the dancers against brilliant orange flames. A cool breeze stirs the leaves of the trees, the waters of the river splash gently along the shores and the ceremony goes on late into the night.

These Pomo Indians are getting ready to dance the sacred Big Head Dance. The Pomos had four or more tribal groups in Lake County who danced the Big Head Dance. There were other tribes on the coast and in the Sacramento Valley who did these dances with their own songs. This photograph was taken in 1907 in Northeastern Colusa County.

BACKTRACKING

Can you answer these questions?

(1) Why are religious ceremonies important to Indian people?

(2) Name three qualities of an Indian leader.

What three qualities would you like to have as a leader?

(3) How did most Indian leaders become the head of their tribe?

(4) What were four duties of the leaders?

(5) Name two types of Indian Doctors and tell about each.

(6) Tobacco was not used daily by the California Indians. How did the Indians use tobacco?

Lanny Pinola is a Pomo-Miwok Indian storyteller and a park ranger at Point Reyes National Park in Northern California. He works with the National Park Service and the California Indian people in his area. During the year, Lanny helps organize California Indian Gatherings at Kule Loklo, the Miwok Village in Point Reyes National Park. He is a leader in the group that sings for the Strawberry Festival, Summer Gatherings, and Big Times. Lanny has also received an honor from the Department of the Interior, the Secretary of the Interior Stewardship Award, in 1991.

CHAPTER TEN
MUSIC, ART, AND GAMES

INDIAN MUSIC

The California Indians have always enjoyed music. Music had and still has a place in every part of Indian life. Singing is the most important part of Indian music. Songs pass on feelings and stories. Songs are handed down from generation to generation.

There is group singing and individual singing at celebrations. There are songs for mourning ceremonies and songs for initiation ceremonies. There are songs for making acorn meal, basketmaking, births, healing, hunting, warfare, and harvesting. Sometimes singing went on for hours and sometimes days.

Most of the time musical instruments accompanied the singing, dancing, and prayers at ceremonies, gatherings, and celebrations. Musical instruments included rattles, clapsticks, whistles, flutes, musical bows, foot drums, and bull roarers. Instruments were made from elderberry wood, bones, reeds, skins, turtle shells, cocoons, deer hooves, and hollow logs. Today clapsticks, whistles, and rattles are still used during many ceremonies.[1]

COCOON, CLAPSTICK, DEER-TOE, AND GOURD RATTLES

Many tribes in California used some type of rattle, such as cocoon-bunch rattles, split clapstick rattles, deer-toe rattles, and **gourd** rattles. One type of rattle was made from dried moth cocoons. In some tribes cocoons were filled with small pebbles and tied to sticks of various lengths.

The second type of rattle was a clapstick about eighteen inches long. The stick was split two-thirds of the way down and tied so it couldn't split anymore. This stick was held in one hand and struck on the palm of the other hand. Men and women kept time to the singing with the clapstick. The clapstick accompanied many kinds of dancing and singing.

The third type of rattle, made of deer toes, was used throughout

California. The Ipai and Tipai Indians of Southern California used the deer-toe rattle as a part of the Mourning Ceremony. Each deer-toe rattle was made to be used only once and was usually burned at the end of the ceremony. Each singer in the Mourning Ceremony made his own deer-toe rattle and only the singers knew how to make them. The gentle clicking of these rattles added a pleasing rhythm to the music of the California Indians.

Some Indians in Southern California such as the Cahuilla and Mojave, used gourds as rattles. Gourds were dried by the Indians. Sometimes small pebbles were placed inside of the gourd. A handle was attached with string made of fiber. Gourd rattles were used in the Cahuilla and Mojave Bird Dances.[2]

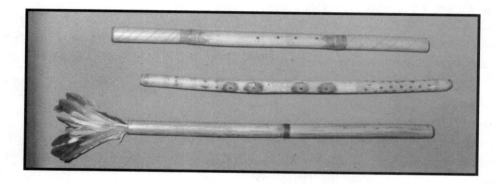

Indian Flutes

WHISTLES, FLUTES, AND MUSICAL BOWS

Whistles were used frequently, especially in dance ceremonies. They were made of bird bones, reed, or cane. To make a whistle, holes were pierced in the bird bones or reeds. Often the whistle was tied on a string and hung around the dancer's neck. As the dancer moved, he could easily put the whistle in his mouth and play it. In some tribes the Indian Doctors blew on a whistle while treating patients.

Flutes were often made of elderberry wood. A flute was an open tube with three or four equally spaced holes. It was blown across the edge of one end. In some tribes such as the Yurok, the flute was used by young men when **courting.** Pomo and Yurok elders sometimes played the flute for pleasure as they sat in front of the sweathouse on quiet, sunny afternoons.

A musical bow was used by the Pomo, Maidu, Yokuts, Ipai, and Tipai Indians. This stringed instrument was modeled after a hunting bow. One end was held in the mouth while the string was tapped. The sound was pleasing and restful and at times was used during **spiritual** ceremonies. Although the flute and musical bow were able to carry **melodies**, they were not used in dance ceremonies probably because the sounds of these instruments did not usually blend well with other instruments and singers' voices.[3]

Using clapsticks, these singers are accompanying dancers with songs and prayers that honor the earth and have been part of California Indian culture for thousands of years. From left to right are Tim Rivera, Tim Rivera's nephew, Bev Marrufo, Jackie Frank, Esther Pinola, and Travis Duncan. They have come to Kule Loklo, the Miwok Village at Point Reyes National Park, to participate in a summer Gathering.

DRUMS

California Indians such as the Pomo, Wintu, Yuki, and Yokuts, used foot drums in their musical expression. A foot drum was large, sometimes six to seven feet long. It was made from a burned-out log and was usually used in the dance house. The foot drum was very sacred to the Indians.

Other Central California Indians used a foot drum that was often a flat wooden plank set over a hole in the floor of the dance house. It was played by a man tapping on it with his foot.

The Hupa, Yurok, and Karuk Indians used a square drum that was smaller than a foot drum. It was made of a cedar wood frame and wrapped with elk skin. Drums were not used in Hupa dances. Drums were used during gambling games.

Sometimes other types of drums were used during games or by an Indian Doctor. The Yurok sometimes tapped a board with a boat paddle. The Maidu, Ipai, and Tipai Indians would strike or rub baskets and the Mojave would tap clay jars. These types of drums were never used as dance drums.[4]

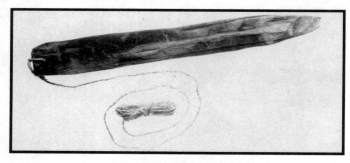

Bull Roarer

BULL ROARER

The **bull roarer**, a slat of wood tied to the end of a thong, made a roaring sound when the thong was whirled by hand. It was used by some tribes in the central part of California such as the Pomo, Yokuts, and Yuki. The bull roarer's whirr, heard during sacred occasions, represented thunder. The Luiseno, Ipai, Tipai, and Mojave Indians in the Southern part of California, used the bull roarer to call people to religious events.

The use of the bull roarer may have been borrowed from the White Mountain Apache Indians in Arizona who made use of the instrument in religious ceremonies. Most of the Northwestern California Indians did not use the bull roarer.[5]

INDIAN ART

The California Indians are proud of their artistic ability. Their beautiful baskets, dance regalia, flaked obsidian blades, abalone shell necklaces, and redwood dug-out canoes are the creations of skilled artists. The California Indians use bone, shell, wood, plant fibers, and other natural products of the environment to pass on traditional designs and patterns that have been inherited from their own native culture.

Baskets of outstanding beauty, feathered headdresses, abalone necklaces polished to perfection, strands of clamshell beads smoothed into disks, soap root brushes washed and combed, a tule doll or an oil painting of a rattlesnake and a hummingbird—are all ways to **communicate** with others through art.[6]

This Yokuts rattlesnake basket is a work of art.

ROCK ART

Rock art is another way the California Indians communicated through art. Designs were painted or cut on rock surfaces and today can be found in many areas of California.

Rock art has been divided into two groups. Designs that were cut or chipped into rocks are called **petroglyphs**. Designs that were painted on rock walls or cliffs are called **pictographs**.

Petroglyphs were made by chipping or pecking the surface of a rock wall or cliff with a smaller, harder stone. Pictographs were painted on the rock surfaces with brushes made from plant fibers and paints made from minerals.

Both men and women made designs on cave walls or other rock surfaces. Petroglyphs and pictographs take the form of human figures, animals, circles, maze-like patterns, wavy lines, and other designs. The meanings of the petroglyphs and pictographs are not always known. Some Indian people and scientists believe that some designs were made by Indian Doctors during ceremonies. Many designs are thought to have been created by hunters.

Thousands of rock drawings or petroglyphs can be found on the walls of ancient basalt cliffs in the Northwestern corner of the Mojave Desert near Ridgecrest, California. This area has more petroglyphs than any other place in California. The Indians who chipped the figures into the cliffs were probably the ancestors of the Panamint-Shoshone Indians living in the Koso Mountains. Big Horn sheep are the most common design, probably because the Koso Indians camped in these canyons to hunt the Big Horns. Other petroglyphs in the canyons include men wearing elaborate clothing and headdresses, dogs, deer, medicine bags, quail, and atlatls. An atlatl is an ancient spear device used long before the bow and arrow. Over hundreds and hundreds of years the Indians have chipped new designs over old designs. This area is now protected by the United States Government.

There are many petroglyph and pictograph sites in California. These sites must be preserved and never damaged. Only a few areas are protected by locked gates. Their locations are usually kept secret by people who know where they are so that **vandals** cannot destroy the rock art. The Park Service of California, the Nature Conservancy and other interested groups such as the Audubon Society as well as individual citizens work hard to protect the rock art of the California Indians.

Today, California Indians continue to show their artistic abilities in their skillfully woven baskets, dug-out canoes, elaborate dance regalia, beautiful shell bead necklaces as well as paintings and sculptures. The art of the California Indians is a part of their heritage. It connects the past with the present and is a part of each person's being.[7]

Vandals have destroyed much of this very old pictograph which was painted by the Indians of Southern California hundreds and hundreds of years ago. The colors in the pictograph are black, brown and red. The meanings of the symbols are not known. If vandals had not destroyed most of this work of art, you would be able to see and appreciate the beauty and wonder of an ancient Indian pictograph. This pictograph is now protected by the Nature Conservancy and the State of California.

Petroglyphs from Little Petroglyph Canyon near Ridgecrest, California

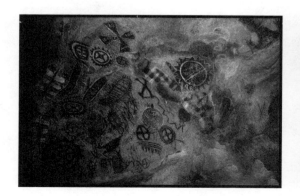 

Pictographs from Painted Cave, Santa Barbara, California

CHILDREN'S GAMES

Children and young people played many types of games. Some games helped them gain skills that they would use later in life. Other games were for fun.

Children's games included hide and seek, tag, broad-jumping, wrestling, foot races, kickball, swimming, diving, jumping rope, and target shooting. Boys played with small bows and arrows and bull roarers. Girls played with dolls made of clay, grass, sticks, or tules. Both boys and girls enjoyed spinning tops made from acorns.

CAT'S CRADLE

Cat's cradle was a string game that children liked to play. The string was made from plant fibers. The string was looped over the wrists and fingers of each hand and passed back and forth between the two hands. Simple loops were done by young beginners. As the person became more skilled he could pick up loops from another person's hands. The Indians had many different patterns that they memorized.[8]

The Cahuilla Indians believed that the cat's cradle game played a role in the journey of the spirit to a place where the spirits of the dead lived.

SHINNY

Shinny was a fast-moving game the Indians played much like hockey. There were many different ways to play shinny. Indian boys learned to play shinny at a very early age. They often hunted for strong branches with knobs on them to use as shinny sticks and a rounded piece of wood or bone to use as a ball or **puck**. To begin the game, the teams stood in the center of the playing field and the ball was put into play. Each team tried to make points by hitting the wooden ball past the other team's goal line. This game was also played by the adults.

Games such as shinny involved strength and constant attention. This type of game was exciting and the players enjoyed the competition with each other.[9]

THE RING-AND-PIN GAME

This game was made with a buckskin thong or heavy fiber string about fifteen inches long. One end of the string was tied to a wooden stick or bone pin. Several rings usually made of salmon or deerbone **vertebrae** were strung on the thong. The thong was knotted at the end so the rings would not slide off the thong. The player tossed the rings into the air and tried to catch as many rings as possible on the stick. Sometimes the rings for this game were made from large acorn caps.

Another version of this game was played by the Chumash. Only one ring was attached to the end of the thong and the player tried to catch the ring on the stick.

Ring-and-pin games were fun for children to play. These games also helped young boys develop their skills for hunting and fishing. The Wailaki, Shasta, Wintu, Patwin, Luiseno, and many other tribes played the ring-and-pin games.[10]

Wailaki ring-and-pin game. The rings are bored deer astragali (ankle bones). Collected in 1901.

THE STICK-AND-HOOP GAME

This game was very popular with boys and young men. It was played with a hoop made from coiled willow branches wrapped with buckskin, tule, or pine bark. It could also be played with a stone disk with a hole in the center. Sometimes the hole in the hoop was only two or three inches across. Each player had a stick or pole and as the hoop was rolled, the players threw their sticks trying to ring the hole in the hoop. It was also played by throwing the pole so it would slide under the rolling hoop. Another version of this game involved shooting arrows through the hoop as it was rolled by the other team.

From early childhood, the young boys played the stick-and-hoop game. This game gave them valuable experience in learning skills that they would later use in hunting and fishing.[11]

Young boys playing the stick-and-hoop game

THE BARK SPINNING GAME

The bark spinning game was played with an oval piece of bark that was threaded through the middle with buckskin thongs. The thongs were twisted and held in each hand. When the person pulled the thongs back and forth, the bark spun around and made a buzzing or humming sound. Sometimes there was a contest between the children playing the game to see whose bark spinner could hum the longest and loudest.[12]

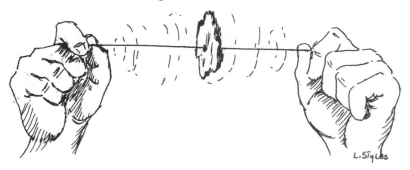

GAMES FOR ADULTS

Games of chance, such as guessing games were games of **mental** strength. They involved skill and quickness of the mind and hands. The Indians were great gamblers and enjoyed this type of competition. Today these games are played at Indian Gatherings throughout California.

The Indians of today enjoy getting together and playing a hand game.

A GUESSING GAME

Indians loved to get together and play guessing games. The game enjoyed by most tribes was the hand or grass game, a contest of guessing. It was played with two bones—one bone was marked. The game was played with two teams, four or more people on each team. They sat facing each other. A pile of counting sticks was placed nearby to keep score. One player held a bone in each hand and would shuffle the bones from hand to hand behind his back or in front of him. A person on the opposite team would then try to guess which hand held the marked bone. Players became expert at changing the bones from one hand to the other and confusing the other team. Sometimes players sang songs to bring good luck to the team. If a player made a correct guess, his team received a counting stick and the bones went to him to continue the game.

This game went on until one team had won all the counting sticks. When one team had all the counters, the game was over. Players and watchers placed bets, used good luck charms and started the game over again. Often this game could go on for days. The rules for this game might be different from tribe to tribe.[13]

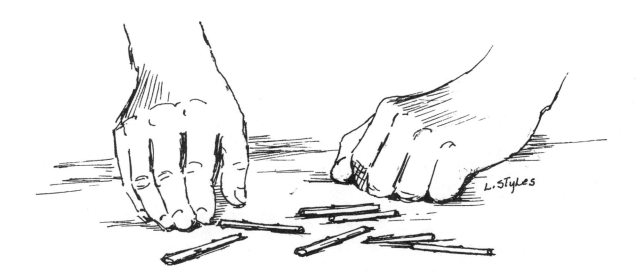

A STAVES GAME

Another popular game among the Indians was a staves game played by women. Three staves or sticks of wood made from willow or elderberry wood were split in half. Designs were made on the rounded sides of the staves and the split sides were left with no design. Three of the staves had the same design. The other three staves sometimes had a different design. A woman player held her set of staves and threw them like dice on the ground. Players made bets on the way the designs would turn up. Counting sticks were used to keep score. There were many ways to play this game. One way to play the game was as follows: counting sticks were placed in a pile. When the staves were thrown, there were only two combinations that counted. If half of the staves landed with flat sides up, it counted as one point. The woman who threw the staves was given one counting stick. If all the staves landed the same way (up or down), it was worth two points and the player was given two counting sticks. No other combinations counted. When all the counting sticks were divided among the players, the game still continued. Each time a player threw a winning combination of staves, she took a counting stick or sticks from the other player. The game was over when one player had all the counting sticks.[14]

Designs were put on game staves by making a design out of bark and holding the bark against the rounded side of the sticks. The sticks were then held over the fire until blackened with soot so that when the bark was removed the design remained.

A DICE GAME

Indian women also played a dice game. The women skillfully made dice for this game from the washed and split shells of the native black walnut. The nut meat was removed from the shells and than each shell was filled with soft pitch or asphaltum. Pieces of abalone shell were pressed into the pitch or asphaltum so that each shell had a different design. Usually the game was played with six or eight shells and counting sticks were used to keep score. The women threw the shells onto a large, flat basket tray. The shells were thrown rapidly and points were given depending on how the shells landed—flat side up or flat side down.[15]

Indians of all ages enjoyed games and contests. When the Indians gathered for ceremonies or celebrations, both children and adults played many types of games. Today, games are still a part of every gathering and celebration.

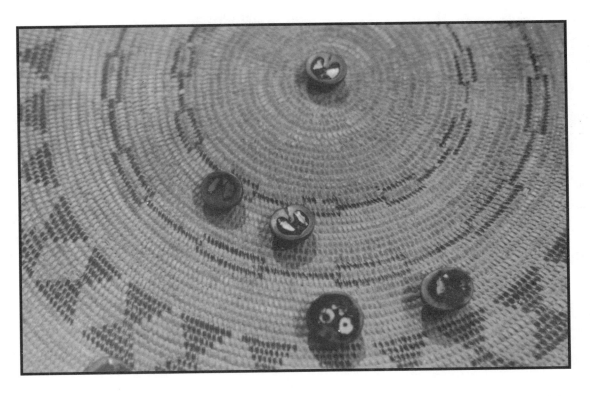

These walnut halves have been filled with pitch or asphaltum and decorated with bright pieces of shell. They were used in a dice game played by women.

INTERESTING THOUGHTS

From cat's cradle to ring-and-pin games, and from foot races to shinny, all boys and girls enjoy games. Many of the games that are played today were first played hundreds and hundreds of years ago by the California Indians. If you have played a good game of hockey, soccer, or football or enjoyed games such as hide and seek, guessing games, or pick-up-sticks, remember that these are some of the types of games that began long ago with the First Californians.

*PLAYGROUNDS

I like playgrounds
Orange and blue playgrounds
High climbing playgrounds
Hide and seek playgrounds
Playgrounds in the woods
I like playgrounds.

Richard Sanderson
Grade 2
Hoopa Elementary School

*1993 Art Connects Literary Magazine. Editors: Atkins, Dr. Amy L., Bucklew, Mary. United States Department of Education Fund for Innovation in Education, 1993.

BACKTRACKING

Can you answer the following questions?

(1) All of the California Indians have songs. They will always have songs. Why are their songs so important?

(2) Name three musical instruments used by the Indians. What materials were used to make each instrument?

(3) Why is art important to the California Indians?

(4) Some games helped children and young people gain skills that they would use later in life. Name two games played by children and tell what skills could be learned from each game.

(5) Name a game that Indian women enjoyed playing. Tell how it was played.

(6) Name one or more games we have today that are borrowed from the Indians. How are these games similar to the Indian games?

Ishi, a special Californian

CHAPTER ELEVEN
ISHI, A SPECIAL CALIFORNIAN

ISHI'S EARLY LIFE

Long before the non-Indians came to California, there lived a tribe of Indian people who called themselves the Yana. The Yana lived in North Central California and were divided into four groups—the Northern Yana, the Central Yana, the Southern Yana, and the Yahi Yana.

Ishi was a Yahi. The Yahi lived in the forests and mountains east of the Sacramento River between Mill and Deer Creeks. The Yahi were a small group of people unlike the Yokuts of the Great Central Valley or the Pomo of Central California who had many, many members in their tribes. The Yahi sometimes fought with neighboring tribes and when they sensed a losing battle, they would return to the protection of the cliffs, canyons, mountains, and dense forests of Deer Creek and Mill Creek.

When Ishi was very young, his first memory of non-Indians was one of hatred. Non-Indians had looted and **ransacked** the Yahi village where he lived and killed his father and other members of his tribe. Because of many killings like this and the fear of more killings, Ishi's small tribe went deeper into the protection of the Deer Creek wilderness. There they lived out of sight of non-Indians for many years.

During this time, Ishi was initiated into the Yahi sweathouse. Here he learned of the Yahi way of life and the ceremonies and traditions that had been passed down in his tribe from generation to generation. Though his tribe had only a few members, the Yahi traditions were still celebrated as in the past. Each year in the fall, Ishi and his people gathered acorns and stored dried fish and meat in handmade baskets for the long winter. Ishi and his family celebrated the harvest season with singing and dancing.

Ishi and his family loved the forests and the meadows. They hunted deer, rabbit, and squirrel. Ishi fished for salmon and trout in the cool, clear streams. At this time Ishi lived in the sweathouse with the other men of the small tribe. In the winter, they lived in his mother's earth-covered home. At the beginning of the twentieth century, who would have guessed that this small group of Yahi Indians, supposedly vanished, was still celebrating age-old customs.

One day, after almost forty years, some surveyors, working for a water company, came upon Ishi's small camp. Ishi and his family ran into the forest to hide. The workers explored the camp and found a very sick old woman. They left her alone, but as the surveyors left the camp, they took the Indians' baskets, rabbit skin blankets, bows and arrows, and tools. The surveyors stole the things that Ishi and his family needed to use everyday. When Ishi returned to the camp, he knew it would take many months to replace the stolen tools and baskets. It would be very hard for the few remaining people of the tribe to survive without these important tools.

Gradually, life began to change for Ishi. Now Ishi and his mother found themselves alone. At his mother's death, Ishi followed the customs of his tribe. He blew tobacco to the four winds, painted mourning stripes across his face, and singed off his hair close to his head. Ishi, starving and lonely, decided to leave the protection of the Deer Creek wilderness. For three years Ishi wandered until he was found one morning on a ranch near Oroville, California.

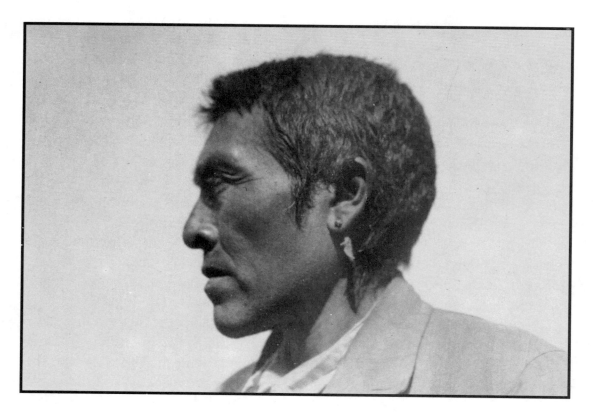

Ishi was in mourning for the loss of his loved ones when he was found in Oroville, California in 1911. He had singed off his hair close to his head as was the Yahi custom when someone died.

ISHI IN THE NON-INDIAN WORLD

It was April, in the year 1911, when Ishi came into the non-Indian world. He was found crumpled against the side of a barn. He had no knife nor bow and arrow. After spending the night in the Oroville jail, Ishi was introduced to a man named A.L. Kroeber. Dr. Kroeber was a college professor who was interested in California Indians. Dr. Kroeber took Ishi to San Francisco to live. He showed Ishi many Indian **artifacts**, some of which had belonged to Ishi's very own tribe.

Ishi learned to wear clothes like the people he saw each day, but he did not like shoes. He shook hands to greet new friends even though this was not his custom. He was not impressed by the tall buildings of San Francisco because he probably compared them in his mind to the high cliffs of the Yahi world where he had grown up. Although Ishi thought that modern inventions such as matches, automobiles, airplanes, and trolley cars were truly **miracles**, what really impressed him were the thousands of people in the city of San Francisco. Never had Ishi seen so many people in one place.

A RETURN TO YAHI COUNTRY

During the five years that Ishi lived in San Francisco, he made one trip back to the Yahi world with Dr. Kroeber and three friends. The men lived as Ishi had lived—hunting with bows and arrows, fishing, taking sweat baths, and gathering berries and seeds. This they did for over a month. Each day they went to a new place where Ishi had lived. As Ishi shared his ways, Dr. Kroeber recorded everything he learned from Ishi. Dr. Kroeber knew that it was important to record and keep Ishi's culture and traditions so that the Yahi way would not be lost forever.[1]

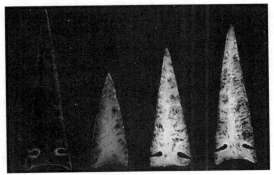

Arrow points made by Ishi

Ishi making a bow

When Ishi went with Dr. Kroeber and a few friends to Yahi country, Ishi showed the men how to make bows and arrows. He also showed them how to hunt for deer and skin the animal.

Ishi showing how to use a bow and arrow

INTERESTING THOUGHTS

When Ishi died in 1916, the world lost a special individual—a man of courage, love, and gentleness. Those people who were fortunate enough to live and talk with Ishi, came to understand the spirit that lives within the Indian—a spirit that is quiet, patient, kind, and sensitive to the world about him.

BACKTRACKING

Can you answer these questions?
(1) Where did Ishi grow up? Can you pinpoint this spot on a California map?

(2) How did Ishi and his family survive without being discovered for so many years?

(3) Why did Ishi leave his mountain home and enter the non-Indian world?

(4) What impressed Ishi the most about the non-Indian world?

(5) Why did Ishi and Dr. Kroeber return to Yahi country? Why did Dr. Kroeber record the ways of Ishi?

Youp-Shreeta-Neetah, meaning "an infant" in the Klamath Indian language, was born in the Klamath River area. Non-Indians called her Mollie Oscar. She married a Shasta Indian leader and became a member of the Shasta tribe by adoption. She is remembered for her kindness to motherless Indian and non-Indian children. This photograph was taken in 1941.

CHAPTER TWELVE

CALIFORNIA INDIANS THEN AND NOW

IN THE BEGINNING

In the beginning, nature whispered its welcome to the First Californians. The Indians accepted the warmth of this greeting and lived in the beauty of the mountains, plains, and deserts of California. The Indians lived in harmony with nature. They valued every animal, rock, and stream that was a part of their surroundings and thanked the Great Spirit/Creator for these gifts. The California Indians respected the environment. They were a part of the land. They understood it and took care of it throughout all generations.

The California Indians lived for thousands and thousands of years as caretakers of the land they had been given. Each person was a member of a highly skilled tribe who lived and worked with the natural environment. From the land, the Indians built homes, made tools, and gathered and hunted food, but they did not change the delicate balance of nature. They did not take more than they needed from the land and with many special ceremonies, they honored the earth with prayers, songs, and dances.

SPANISH INVADERS

One day a Spanish ship loomed on the California horizon. The size of the ship, the billowing white sails, and the sunlight gleaming off the metal helmets of the Spaniards were strange sights for the Indians to behold. Armor-clad men came ashore and claimed all the land, rivers, lakes, deserts, and mountains for the King of Spain. The Spanish did not honor the Indians as the rightful owners of the land. The land became Spanish territory and the Indians became citizens of New Spain.[1]

With the coming of Spanish padres and soldiers in 1769, there were approximately 310,000 Indians living in California. The padres came to **convert** the Indians to the Christian religion. They wanted to show the

Indians how to live, eat, and dress like Europeans, how to farm and how to pray to the Christian God. The soldiers came to protect the padres and claim more land for the Spanish.

From 1769 to 1823, missions were built and for over fifty years, thousands of Indians from San Diego to Sonoma became **neophytes**, new church members, in the chain of twenty-one missions.

The Spanish padres forced the Indians to learn the Spanish way of life. The padres felt that if the Indians stayed with them as **apprentices** for ten years, the Indians would be able to teach other Indians the Spanish way of life. The Spanish promised the Indians that when they learned the Spanish ways, the land would be given to them.[2]

For more than sixty-five years the lives of all the neophytes at the missions were regulated by the ringing of mission bells that called the Indians to work and worship.

Most of the Indians were not happy at the missions. They were forced to build the mission buildings and **presidios**. The Indians planted the crops and tended the herds of animals. Without the Indians' work, the missions would have failed.

Often daily life at the missions was miserable for the Indians. As early as 1786, visitors from other countries wrote that the Indians were brought to the missions by force. Foreign visitors also noted that the Indians were not allowed to leave the missions and suffered harsh punishment at the hands of the soldiers.[3]

SPAIN LOSES CALIFORNIA TO MEXICO

In 1821, Spain lost a war with Mexico. By 1834, sixty-five years after the mission chain had been started, Spain no longer owned the land of California. Now, the Mexican flag flew over California. Many padres left California and the missions were sold or **abandoned**. There had been 81,000 Indians taken into the twenty-one missions and over 60,000 Indians had died. Epidemics of **smallpox**, **diphtheria**, and measles had killed thousands of Indians.[4] There remained about 15,000 Indian neophytes. These Indians no longer were under the rule of the mission padres.

Most of the Indians were never given the land that had been promised to them. Some of those who did receive small pieces of land lost the land to people who cheated them. For example, Ynigo, an Ohlone leader, applied to the Mexican government for a land grant in 1844. He received 1,700 acres in the San Francisco Bay Area. By 1881, after California became a state, Ynigo's land grant was given to the owners of the New Almaden Mine. In nearby Santa Clara, 2,200 acres of land were granted to two Ohlone Indians. Again, after California became a state, the land was given to the first United States postmaster of the town of San Jose.[5]

In Vista, California, Rancho Guajome stands on land that was an Indian rancheria long before non-Indians arrived. There were many frog ponds on the land. The Indians named the area Wakhavumi, which means "Frog Pond."

In 1798 when San Luis Rey Mission was built, Wakhavumi became mission land. Later the Spanish called the area Guajome, their pronunciation of the Indian name. In 1845 when the Mexican government took over the mission lands, Governor Pio Pico granted Guajome to two Indian brothers, Jose and Andres Manuel. The brothers owned the two thousand acres for a short time before they decided to sell the land to Mr. Abel Stearns of Los Angeles for $550.00. Mr. Abel Stearns gave the land as a wedding gift to his wife's sister, Ysabel Bandini, daughter of Juan Bandini of San Diego when she married Cave Couts, an American Lieutenant of the First Dragoons. Couts built the rancho adobe in 1852. (This information courtesy of Mary F. Ward, Historian, County of San Diego, Department of Parks and Recreation.)

Other Indians who had left the missions, went to live as laborers, servants, and **vaqueros** on the Mexican ranchos. Life on the ranchos and in the Mexican towns was difficult for the Indians. The towns were not healthy places for the Indians and many died of diseases. Many Indians lost all contact they had with their tribal groups and some Indians no longer had their own culture or traditions.[6]

Those Indians who returned to their native villages, found many of their villages gone. Diseases had caused the death of thousands and thousands of Indians who had never been taken into the mission system. In one epidemic during the early 1830s, fur trappers from the north had been in contact with trading ships from Hawaii. Fur trappers caught **malaria** from the Hawaiians and carried malaria into the Sacramento area. Complete villages of Indians up and down the Sacramento River area were destroyed because of this rapid-spreading disease. Villages were also destroyed by raids and killings carried out by the Mexican soldiers and settlers.[7] Because of the senseless murders and terrible diseases, the Indian population continued to get smaller and smaller.

THE INDIANS AND THE GOLD RUSH

By 1848, the Indian population had been reduced from 310,000 to 100,000.[8] With the discovery of gold, more hardships and cruelties were in store for the Indians. Gold miners began to flood into California. Miners swarmed the foothills and streams of Northern California looking for gold. Stories of fabulous riches spread to all corners of the world and as California became world-known, more and more miners came.

Once again the Indian lands were overrun by people who paid no attention to boundary claims of the Indians. Some Indians were forced to work in the gold fields for non-Indian miners. They received no money for their work and were paid with food and clothing. Other Indians agreed to work for non-Indian miners for payment. Still other Indians mined for gold on their own and traded their gold for food and other goods.[9] A government report in 1848 said that more than half of the gold diggers in the California mines were Indians.[10] Many Indians, however, were cheated out of the gold they mined with worthless items such as glass beads, cloth, or strong drink.[11] By 1849, shootings and violent deaths of the Indians forced the Indians who survived to stop mining for gold.[12]

Soon settlers came to California. Once again the Indians' rights of liberty and private property were ignored. As the settlers pushed into the Indian lands, Indian villages were attacked, the people killed, and the land taken by the settlers. Land, plants, and animals were recklessly destroyed by the settlers. The food sources of the Indians were destroyed and the Indians were unable to gather foods on their traditional lands.[13]

Goldminers and settlers took over the land of the Indians.

CALIFORNIA BECOMES A STATE

In October 1849, California and American **delegates** gathered in Monterey, California. They were to decide on the rules and government duties for the new state of California. Many delegates wanted to keep Indians from voting. The delegates felt that only white males over 21 years of age could vote. Indians were not given voting rights or citizenship rights.[14] After California had been admitted to the Union in 1850, new laws did not allow the Indians to testify in court or to carry firearms.[15] Sadly, most Indians had to wait almost 75 years before they could become citizens and vote in California.[16]

In 1850, the California legislature adopted a law calling Indians **vagabonds** if they did not have jobs. Because of this law, Indians could be arrested and fined. If they could not pay their fine, they could be sold as workers to the highest bidder.[17]

In 1851, three commissioners for the United States government signed 18 treaties with 139 Indian tribes in California. These treaties meant that the Indians would be removed from mining areas and other areas where settlers were taking Indian land. The Indians would be moved to large **reservations** to protect the Indians and to free Indian land for the use of settlers. The United States Congress would not agree to these treaties because they were against giving so much land to the Indians! The Indians who had already moved to the new reservations were left without their home lands and now they had no reservation lands.[18]

In 1852, smaller reservation lands were set aside for the Indians. Army forts were located nearby. Food for the Indians was always in short supply, the soldiers at the army forts did not protect the Indians, and money for the Indians from the United States government went into the pockets of dishonest agents of the **Bureau of Indian Affairs**.[19]

One of the first Indian reservations to be started was the Round Valley Indian Reservation in 1856. Round Valley was the traditional homeland of the Yuki Indian people. Indians from other tribes were brought by force to the Round Valley Reservation. The Konkow, Maidu, some Pomo, Nomlaki, Cahto, Wailaki, Pit River, and Yuki peoples were forced to live together. At first, there were many problems. The Yuki who were the original inhabitants of Round Valley had to share their home with other Indians who spoke different languages, lived with other beliefs, and used the land and its resources differently. After many years, the descendants formed a new tribe on the reservation, the Covelo Indian Community, also known as the Confederated Tribes of Round Valley.[20]

Round Valley near Ukiah, California

THE BUREAU OF INDIAN AFFAIRS

When the Constitution of the United States was adopted in the year 1788, the thirteen original states gave the federal government the responsibility of working with Indian tribes. The group of men in the United States government who worked with the Indians became known as the War Department. In 1824 the men in this department decided to rename their group the Bureau of Indian Affairs. Today, if an Indian wishes to have the services of the Bureau of Indian Affairs, he or she must live on a reservation or must have Indian heritage from a tribe or group of Indians recognized by the government of the United States. Some Indian tribes are not **federally** recognized by the United States government. Recently Public Law Number 10246 was passed in the 103rd Congress to work on this problem.

In 1849 the Bureau of Indian Affairs became a part of the **Department of the Interior** of the United States government and remains in that department to this day. In July 1993, a new Assistant Secretary for Indian Affairs was appointed by the President of the United States. This new Assistant Secretary is Ada Deer, an American Indian from the Menominee Indian tribe in Wisconsin. As part of her duties, Ada Deer is also the Commissioner of the Bureau of Indian Affairs and oversees the work of that department.[21]

Ada E. Deer is the first woman to be Assistant Secretary for Indian Affairs in the United States Department of the Interior, Washington, D.C.

The words below are parts of a statement that Ada Deer made to the Senate Committee on Indian affairs on July 15, 1993. She gave this statement when she was nominated for the office of Assistant Secretary for Indian Affairs in the United States Department of the Interior, Washington, D.C.

"Mr. Chairman, Mr. Vice-Chairman and other members of the Senate Committee on Indian Affairs, my name is Ada Elizabeth Deer and I am proud to say I am an enrolled member of the Menominee Indian Tribe of Wisconsin. I am honored that the President and the Secretary of the Interior have nominated me as the first woman to be Assistant Secretary for Indian Affairs. . . .

. . .I was born on the Menominee Indian Reservation in Wisconsin, a land of dense forests, a winding wild river, and streams and lakes that nourish the land, animals, and the people. I am an extension of this environment that has fostered my growth and enriched my vision. An appreciation and reverence for the land is fundamental to being Indian.

Our family of seven lived in a log cabin on the banks of the Wolf River. We had no running water or electricity. Yet, while all of the statistics said we were poor, I never felt poor in spirit. . . .

. . .In time, I graduated from the University of Wisconsin, where I received a wonderful education and which was supported by a tribal scholarship. I then attended Columbia University and received a Masters in Social Work. I was drawn to social work for it embodies many Indian values and it is dedicated to social justice and the elimination of discrimination.

. . .Although Indians now constitute 90 percent of the employees in the Bureau of Indian Affairs, we must remember that the Bureau was created by non-Indians. It has not been a proactive Indian institution. I want to activate and to mobilize people in the Bureau of Indian Affairs so that they can be creative and forward-looking. I want the Indian values of sharing, caring, and respect incorporated into their day-to-day work. I want to help the Bureau of Indian Affairs be a full partner in the effort to fulfill the Indian agenda. The best way we can do this is for the tribes to decide what needs to be done and for the tribes to do it on their own terms, with the Bureau of Indian Affair's support.

. . .We think most of all about the future of our young people. On this summer night tens of thousands of girls and boys across Indian country will go to sleep. Some in my Wisconsin home land will hear the sounds I heard many years ago in the cabin where I grew up. Others will hear the wind in the Douglas fir trees at Warm Springs, the great waters of the Missouri at Fort Peck, or the song of the canyon wren calling out from a redrock monument at Navajo. There is no reason why the children cannot grow up to live in prosperity, in good health, with excellent educations, in clean environments, and immersed in their rich traditions.

...If we work together, I am sure that we can take away the barriers of the past, and work with the tribes to welcome the twenty-first century.

In closing, know that I bring a strong sense of history, vision, maturity, and compassion to the job before me.

Thank you very much."

CALIFORNIA INDIAN RESERVATIONS AND RANCHERIAS

Many California Indians live on reservations, land granted to them by the federal government of the United States. Reservations are areas of land reserved for Indian use. Every active reservation in California has a governing body. The governing body of the tribe is generally referred to as the **tribal council**. It is made up of men and women elected by the vote of the adult members of the tribe and is led by the tribal **chairperson** or **spokesperson**. The tribal council has the authority to speak and act for the tribe. It also has the authority to represent the tribe in dealings with federal, state, and local government.

There is also land in California that is bought by the federal government and given to the Indians as tribal lands. These lands are called **rancherias**. Sometimes rancheria land is purchased by Indians on their own. The government does not own rancheria land.[22]

As you look down from Andreas Canyon high in the San Jacinto Mountains, you can see Palm Springs far below. The Agua Caliente Band of Cahuilla Indians who live on this reservation have lived here in the canyons and valleys for centuries. Long ago the Indians spent the summers in the cool canyons of the mountains where there was wild game, berries, and cool water. In the winter months, the Cahuillas moved to the desert floor where there were and still are the warm waters of mineral springs.

Anthony Andreas and his wife Sally live in Banning, California. Anthony is the head singer of the Agua Caliente Cahuilla Indian Bird Singers. Anthony's group has 18 members and the dancers are from the Palm Springs Indian Reservation and the Morongo Indian Reservation in Banning.

The Bird Singers dance in many places. Their dances tell the Cahuilla tribal history. They dance for the community and for special events in public and private schools, Gatherings, and Pow-Wows.

The head singers wear regular clothes for all performances, which are Levi's, a ribbon shirt, and a cowboy hat with a neckerchief about the neck. The men dancers also wear ribbon shirts. The women wear printed cotton ribbon dresses and capes. These traditional outfits are based on photographs taken in the 1900s.

These Cahuilla Bird Singers are from the Palm Springs and Morongo Indian Reservations in Southern California. The songs of the Cahuilla men tell the stories of the Cahuilla people and their travels in ancient times. From left to right the singers are Tony Andreas, John Andreas, Joshua Andreas, Anthony Andreas, Matt Pablo, Jean Pablo, and Rob Neccochea. This photograph was taken in 1978.

INDIAN POPULATION

The April 1990 United States **Census** reported that living in California's 58 counties, there are 242,162 American Indians. Of this Native American Indian population, 36,511 are California Indians living on 98 reservations and rancherias. There are also many California Indians living in cities and towns throughout California that the census was not able to count. Indians who do not live on reservations, but who belong to federally recognized tribes are able to receive health, housing and education benefits as well as other benefits from the federal government.[23]

INDIAN EDUCATION

Today, all children in California are required to go to school. Many Indian children attend public or private schools. Many Indian children attend schools on federally recognized reservations. Some Indian children attend boarding schools managed by the Bureau of Indian Affairs.

In 1919, only 2,199 Indian children were enrolled in public schools. In 1934, the Johnson-O'Malley Act was passed by the federal government. Although this bill has been changed many times, its main purpose is to guarantee that Indian children have educational opportunities they may not otherwise receive. Money from the Johnson-O'Malley fund pays for the **unique** needs of Indian children in public schools and Indian Education Centers. Johnson-O'Malley funds are used in public schools and Indian Education Centers to teach Indian children language, reading, mathematics, science, Indian arts, Indian culture, and other educational activities.[24]

> ### *I AM UNIQUE
> My full name is Lance Lee McCovey. My ethnic heritage is Hupa. I can speak two languages, English and Hupa. The three things I like are football, baseball and hunting. The person who is nicest to me is my mom. I try to be nicest to grandma and mom. I am the happiest when I go hunting. I am saddest when I get yelled at. My favorite food is hamburger.
>
> Lance McCovey
> Grade 5
> Hoopa Elementary School

*1993 Art Connects Literary Magazine. Editors: Atkins, Dr. Amy L., Buckelew, Mary. United States Department of Education Fund for Innovation in Education, 1993.

Andrew Andreoli is a Hupa Indian. He lives on the Hoopa Reservation in Hoopa, California. Andrew is the Director of the Indian Teacher Education Personnel Program at Humboldt State University in Northern California.

Andrew says, "A good education allows one to become free, free to explore the vast amount of knowledge about our tribal traditions and cultures stored in books and in oral traditions of the elders. Through this way we will continue to be Indians forever."

Nancy DiMaggio and her mother, Mrs. Loretta Head, are Pomo Indians. Nancy is a Certified Massage Therapist in Walnut Creek, California, and works with the body, mind, and spirit of her clients. Nancy's occupation carries on the skills that she feels have been passed on to her from her grandmother.

Mrs. Head, Nancy's mother, has shared the heritage of her people with family, friends, and classroom students. Mrs. Head remembers her young life on a rancheria near the Russian River in Northern California. She also remembers being sent away to Sherman Boarding School in Riverside, California when she was a young child. Mrs. Head enjoys watching her daughter, Nancy, dance at traditional Indian Gatherings and she, too, sometimes takes part in a dance.

Nancy DiMaggio has written these thoughts to honor her elders.

Honoring of The Elders, Keepers of Wisdom

As I gaze into the photographs of the Elder's faces that are a part of my family; and, I ponder the many wonderful Elders I have met in my growing years; and, still hold that I am so very fortunate to live in the presence of a very dear and loving Elder, my Mother, I think of the many , many teachings I have learned from all of them, simply by being in their presence. I watched and accepted my Mother subtly weave these teachings into my life simply by her living the "Ways," that were most important to our People, in order to strengthen my character, personality and spirituality. My heart can only speak the words of truth by expressing the many "thank yous" that are due to all the Elders for the Ways that they have kept alive, in spite of all their hardships. And so, dear ones, Thank you for

> Your unfailing Strength,
> Your stories of Wisdom,
> Your songs of Beauty,
> Your knowledge of the food of the Earth,
> Your hands that wove many Pomo baskets of intricate Beauty,
> Your eyes that found the Healing Plants,
> Your knowledge of how to live in Balance with all things,
> Your dedication to good work and works of Goodness,
> Your ability to Share Freely,
> Your soft and healing hands with so much Loving Strength,
> Your knowledge of the Great Circle of Life as taught in the Pomo Round House and the
>   honoring of the Sacred Directions,
> And most of all your ability to always have kept your attentiveness to the Creator and
>   the Ways that have preserved our People.

These, my dear friends, are but a few words of gratitude in which to honor our Elders. Perhaps one day many will know and understand the Beauty that the Elders bridge with those who follow in their teachings. And perhaps, one day many will honor their Knowing as they pass these precious gifts of respect on to the Youth of tomorrow. Idoshanl - Ho!

—Nancy DiMaggio

Lenette Justina Saubel, the little girl on the right front cover of this book, is now 20 years old. She is a Cahuilla Indian and lives in Palm Springs, California. Lenette is working at the Bureau of Indian Affairs, but her goal is to work in office administration or in child development. Lenette started dancing when she was five years old and stopped at the age of eight. Lenette learned much about tribal dances and this helped her understand and accept different races of people and their cultures.

Howard Chavez is a Pomo Indian from the Big Valley and Sulphur Bank Rancherias of Lake County, California. He graduated from Lower Lake High School, then Humboldt State University, finally returning to Konocti Unified School District as a teacher, where he taught history and mathematics for nine years. After graduating from the University of San Francisco, he became the principal of Round Valley High School on the Round Valley Indian Reservation in 1990. In addition, he started the Round Valley Continuation High School in 1991. There are 126 students at the high school and 18 students at the Continuation High School. Over fifty percent of the students at Round Valley High School and Round Valley Continuation School are American Indians. Howard works at building positive relationships with his students. Howard started the first annual "Honoring Elders Day" at Round Valley High School and Round Valley Continuation High School in 1993.

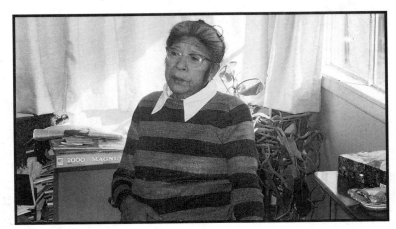

Jane Penn is a Wanakik-Cahuilla Indian from the Morongo Reservation in Banning, California. In 1965 she started the Malki Indian Museum on the Morongo Reservation. This museum displays California Indian baskets and artifacts and publishes books about Indian culture. Jane Penn was appointed to the California Native American Heritage Commission in 1977. She worked hard to preserve and protect all California Indian culture and traditions. Jane died in 1980, but her memory will remain forever.

Antoinette Flora Saubel, the little girl on the left front cover of this book, is now 19 years old. She is a Cahuilla Indian and lives in Banning, California.

My name is Antoinette Flora Saubel and I'm part of the Agua Caliente Band of Cahuilla Indians of Palm Springs, California. I am nineteen years old and I am a proud Cahuilla Bird Dancer. I have been dancing since I was four years old and will remain doing so forever. My step-father, Anthony J. Andreas, is the head singer of our group and he is the person who has kept me so strong in my dancing. Our group consists of eighteen members and we are all "one" family. The dancers are either from the Palm Springs Indian Reservation or the Morongo Indian Reservation in Banning. We dance in many areas and places, whether it be for the community or special events, such as dancing for public or private schools, Girl/Boy Scouts, Pow-Wows, birthdays, and funerals. We don't dress in our traditional wear for all events, just for certain performances and occasions. If we are not wearing our traditional wear, then we are in our modern day clothing. Our singers basically wear regular clothes for all performances, which is Levi's and a shirt. Same for the head singers, only they wear a ribbon shirt and some bead work. As for the girls, we wear cotton dresses with a floral print on the material and ribbon sewn all around the border of the cape and we wear beaded work and jewelry. The only musical instrument that we use is the gourd rattle.

The Cahuilla Bird Songs tell the story of my Cahuilla ancestors migrating from our home in Palm Springs to Mexico looking for better land for hunting and living. Later, my ancestors realized the better area was their home in Palm Springs and that's where we have remained — from then until now!

I am proud to be a Cahuilla Indian and love to dance to the Cahuilla Bird Songs. I participate in many other events and activities that will help my people and other Indian tribes. I have been the president for four years of the Indian Club at Banning High School. I was also student representative for the Title IV representatives for all the Indian students who attended public schools under the Banning School District. I attended a summer program in 1991 for Indian students in the 9th and 12th grade in Irvine, California called N.A.I.U.P.* In 1992 I went back to Irvine for the program, but I went back as a peer assistant which is basically a counselor for the students. I am on a committee for my tribe to build a day-care center for our children.

I am proud to say that I have done things for myself and for the benefit of others and I will continue to do so by furthering my education and helping my tribal people and other tribes as well. After all, we Native American Indians have to stick together in order to keep our spirit, culture, and traditions alive, otherwise our heritage and all that we have conquered will be lost forever.

—Antoinette Saubel

---

*N.A.I.U.P. stands for **Native American Intertribal University Preparatory** summer program at the University of California, Irvine, California.

CALIFORNIA INDIANS TODAY

How did the California Indians survive the years of population decline, disease, starvation, and violence? Their courage and quiet ways in the face of people flooding into their lands were events that only the strongest spirit could survive. But survive they did.[25]

Today many California Indians preserve their traditions by teaching their children the history, customs, songs, dances, and ceremonies that have been passed down from generation to generation. Many tribes throughout California hold special Gatherings, and Big Times during the year.

California Indians are proud of their traditions and their religious beliefs. Families, friends, and elders gather together to be a part of traditional songs and dances. Indians come from great distances to see their friends and relatives in beautiful regalia, dancing in traditional ceremonies. In their ceremonies, they ask for peace and balance in their world and seek connection with the Great Spirit. Indian traditions haven't died nor have they stood still. They have existed uninterrupted from past to present. Do not talk as if the California Indians are gone. They are here forever.

Northern California children waiting to dance at a Gathering in 1978. These children are learning the ways of their tribe through song and dance.

BACKTRACKING

Can you answer the following questions?

1. How did the missions change the California Indian way of life?

2. What happened to the property rights of the Indians when the Spanish came into California? What happened to the property rights of the Indians when the gold miners came into California? What happened to the property rights of the Indians when the Americans came into California?

3. What would you think if you woke up one morning and found a stranger camping on your land? The stranger announces, "I've come to live on your property!" How would you feel? How do you think the California Indians felt when strangers started to settle on their land?

At a Gathering, these young Cahuilla girls are taking part in a traditional dance. They are from left to right Paula Andreas, Karen Neccochea, Cindy Rice, and Anna Patencio. Photographed in 1978.

PHOTOGRAPH CREDITS

Chapter One: p. 17, The Times—Standard Newspaper, Eureka, CA, Sunday, May 9,1993, photo by Cheryle Easter; p. 19, Natural History Museum of Los Angeles County.

Chapter Two: p. 22, Nancy Richardson, Trinidad, CA; p.29, Phoebe A. Hearst Museum of Anthropology, University of California at Berkeley; p. 30, The Oakland Museum.

Chapter Three: p. 32, Phoebe A. Hearst Museum of Anthropology, University of California at Berkeley; p. 37, The Smithsonian Institution, Washington, D.C.; p. 38, 39, photos taken by Michele Lasagna at The Oakland Museum; p. 40, photo taken by Allen Faber at the San Diego Museum of Man.

Chapter Four: p. 56, photo taken by Allen Faber at the Southwest Museum, Los Angeles, CA.

Chapter Five: p. 98, Phoebe A. Hearst Museum of Anthropology, University of California at Berkeley; p. 99, Ralph Harris, Sun Valley, Idaho; p. 104, 105, 109,Phoebe A. Hearst Museum of Anthropology, University of California at Berkeley.

Chapter Six: p. 114, Janet Caron-Owens, Bright Image; p. 117, Vivien Hailstone, Redding, CA; p.120, The Oakland Museum; p. 122,Phoebe A. Hearst Museum of Anthropology, University of California at Berkeley; p. 123, photo taken by Michele Lasagna at the Malki Museum, Inc., Basket donated by Mrs. F. W. Percival; p. 125, Agua Caliente Cultural Museum, Palm Springs, CA; p. 126 (bottom), 127,Phoebe A. Hearst Museum of Anthropology, University of California at Berkeley; p. 128, The Daily Review, Hayward, CA; p. 130-131 (bottom), San Diego Museum of Man; p. 133, Linda Yamane, Seaside, CA.

Chapter Seven: p. 134, Siskiyou County Museum, Yreka, CA; p. 135, The Oakland Museum; p. 137, photo taken by Allen Faber at the Nevada State Museum, Carson City; p. 142, 143,Phoebe A. Hearst Museum of Anthropology, University of California at Berkeley; p. 145, Ronda Marshall and Cassy Chavez, Hoopa, CA.

Chapter Eight: p. 150, Frank F. Latta Collection; p. 153 (bottom), 156, 161,Phoebe A. Hearst Museum of Anthropology, University of California at Berkeley.

Chapter Nine: p, 169,Phoebe A. Hearst Museum of Anthropology, University of California at Berkeley; p. 171, Siskiyou County Museum, Yreka, CA; p. 173, Frank F. Latta Collection; p. 181, San Diego Museum of Man; p. 183, 184,Phoebe A. Hearst Museum of Anthropology, University of California at Berkeley.

Chapter Ten: p. 188, photo taken by Allen Faber at the San Diego Museum of Man; p. 190, 191, 195, 196, 200,Phoebe A. Hearst Museum of Anthropology, University of California at Berkeley; p. 201, photo taken by Michele Lasagna at the Oakland Museum.

Chapter Eleven: p. 204, 206, 207, 208 (top and bottom), 209,Phoebe A. Hearst Museum of Anthropology, University of California at Berkeley.

Chapter Twelve: p. 212, Siskiyou County Museum, Yreka, CA; p. 220, Jon Holtshopple and Associates, Madison, Wisconsin.

All photos not otherwise credited are the property of Magpie Publications.

All illustrations, sketches, and maps are the property of Magpie Publications.

Composition by California Concepts, San Leandro, CA.

Printing by Blaco Printers, Inc., San Leandro, CA.

GLOSSARY

This glossary gives the meanings of words only as they are used in this book. You may wish to use a dictionary to find other meanings for these words.

abandoned: left alone; deserted; leaving a person or thing

abundantly: plentiful; more than necessary; well supplied

adze: an ax-like tool with a curved blade used for trimming and smoothing wood

agave: a fleshy-leaved plant used for food and fiber

apprentices: persons who must work for another for a certain length of time to learn a trade, skill, or business

archeological sites: places or plots of land where evidence of ancient human life and culture has been found and studied

arrowheads: the pointed, removable tips of arrows made of obsidian, flint, chert, or stone

arrowshaft: the slender stem of an arrow

artifacts: objects such as simple tools, weapons, etc. made by human workmanship and of historical interest

awls: small pointed tools for making holes in wood or leather

barbs: sharp points curving in an opposite direction from the main point of a fishhook, spear, arrow, etc.

basalt: a dark, tough, dense rock often found in a lava flow

Bering Strait: a narrow passage between Alaska and the Soviet Union in Asia connecting the Bering Sea and the Arctic Ocean

Big Times: a Gathering or festival where the California Indians come together to celebrate a special event with prayers, dancing, singing, feasting, games, etc.

botanist: a person who studies about plants

breechcloth: a piece of buckskin hung front and back from the waist by a strip of leather called a thong; a part of an Indian man's clothing

bull roarer: a slat of wood tied to the end of a thong and when whirled, makes a roaring sound

burden: something that is carried; a load

Bureau of Indian Affairs: a department in the United States Government that works with the Indians

cedar: a tall tree in the pine family having clusters of needle-like leaves, cones, and strong wood with a fragrance

census: the counting of the people (population) of a certain area

ceremonial: action or rites such as dances and songs connected with a special occasion, usually a religious occasion; a ceremony

chairperson: a person who is the head of a council or committee

characteristics: features, qualities, or traits of a person that make a person special such as strength, leadership, intelligence, etc.

charmstones: carved stones that have special powers

chert: a hard stone made mostly of quartz or silica that comes in colors of blue, gray, green, and red

chia: a plant that grows in much of California and produces small black seeds used as food and medicine

cinnabar: a heavy, bright red mineral that forms crystals or masses in the ground; the main ore of mercury

citric acid: a substance found in citrus fruits such as lemons and limes

clefts: openings such as cracks or crevices

communal: belonging to or sharing with a group of people; owned by more than one person

communicate: to make something known; to pass along or to share something with others

conifers: trees such as pine, spruce, fir, cedar, yew, and cypress that produce cones

continent: any of the main large land masses or areas of the earth, Africa, Asia, Australia, Europe, North America, South America, and Antarctica

convert: to change from one way or belief to another

courting: trying to gain love or affection

creation stories: stories or accounts that tell how something began or started

cremated: burned to ashes

cultivated: tilled or prepared land for planting seeds or crops

cunning: clever; sly; crafty

dau: a break or change in a pattern

deceased: dead; recently dead

delegates: persons who represent other people and may speak or act for others at meetings, conventions, etc.

delicacy: a choice food; something very pleasing and appealing

dentalium: a shellfish or mollusk that is found in the ocean and has a shell that looks like a long tooth; shells highly prized by the Northwestern California Indians

Department of the Interior: a part of the United States Government that works with the American Indians and is responsible for the nation's natural resources such as forests, parks, fish and game, water, gas, oil, etc.

diagnosed: recognizing or knowing a disease by its signs, symptoms, or characteristics

dialects: forms or varieties of spoken languages that are common to a region, group, or community

diatomaceous earth: earth or soil formed mainly from shells

diphtheria: a dangerous, infectious disease of the throat that brings on weakness, high fever, and forms membranes in air passages that hinder breathing

disguise: to change the appearance or way something looks so that it is not recognized

disk: a thin, flat, round form or shape

double bladed paddle: a pole with a paddle or flat piece of wood, etc. at either end, used to paddle or steer a canoe or boat

drought: a long period of dry weather; lack of rain

dug-out: a boat or canoe made by hollowing out a log

ecologists: persons who study living things and their relationship to the environment

edible: anything that may be eaten; food

elders: older, important people of a family, tribe, community, or group

excavated: uncovered by digging; unearthed

extended family: a family and close relatives living together or nearby each other

fast: to eat very little or nothing

feasting: eating a large, fancy meal usually to celebrate a special event; a celebration or festival

federally: having to do with the government

ferocious: fierce; cruel; threatening; wild and untamed

fibrous: made of a thread-like substance that is often tough and adds strength

foreshaft: the front section or part of a spear or arrow

framework: a structure or support built to hold something together; a basic skeletal structure on which something is built

Gatherings: a get-together or festival where the California Indians meet to celebrate a special event with prayers, dancing, singing, feasting, games, etc.

generation: people who were born and lived during the same period of time with the same beliefs, attitudes, etc.; average period between generations about 30 years

geological: having to do with the study and history of the earth including the earth's crust and interior, rock types, fossils, etc.

geomorphological dating: finding the age of the earth's land forms, fossils, etc.

gourd: the dried, hollow shell of a squash or pumpkin-like fruit

granaries: structures made of twigs, brush, mud, etc., built by the California Indians to store acorns and seeds

haliotis: the family or genus to which abalone, a shellfish, belongs; abalone shells

hammerstone: a stone used like a hammer

hand pump drill: a drill or tool worked by hand with a sharp point to pierce holes in shells, steatite, wood, etc.

hemp: a plant used for the tough fiber in its stem to make rope, cord, or thread

images: copies, imitations, or likenesses of persons or things

Indian hemp: see hemp

inherited: received from a parent, relative, or ancestor upon their death

initiation: ceremonies or special instructions when someone becomes an adult or joins a group or club

intermediate: between two places, things, or stages; in the middle

jasper: a stone consisting of quartz usually reddish, brown, or yellow in color; a variety of quartz

kernels: grain or seeds of corn, wheat, etc.; the inner, soft part of a nut or acorn

kishumnawat: a Cahuilla Indian ceremonial house

latticework: an openwork structure made of crossed strips of wood or branches

leached: pouring water over a substance to wash away or remove a bad taste; filtered or washed away by water

lean-tos: open structures with brush covered flat tops or roofs to keep out the sun

life zones: areas of land that differ from each other according to climate, geography, animal, and plant life

malaria: a disease that causes severe chills and fever and is transferred to humans by the bite of an infected mosquito; a highly infectious disease

marrow: the soft tissue that is found in the inside of bones

mature: full grown; fully developed; ripened

melodies: tones or sounds arranged to make a pleasing tune or song; the leading part of a song

mental: having to do with the mind; intellect

mesquite: a thorny tree or shrub common in Southern California that produces a bean-like edible pod used as food

midden: an area where unneeded materials are piled; shell mounds

middleman: a trader who buys goods from one person and sells the goods to another person; a go-between

milkweed fiber: the string-like threads of a slender plant that grows throughout California

mortar: a bowl made of stone in which seeds, acorns, or herbs are pounded into a powder with a pestle

natural resources: forms of wealth made by nature such as coal, oil, water, land, forests, wildlife, etc.

navigated: to steer or direct a boat or ship

neophytes: persons who are new members of a church or religion; newly baptized into a church

nettle: a plant with tooth-shaped leaves and covered with tiny hairs that give out a stinging fluid creating a rash on contact with skin; a plant used for its fiber to make rope, thread, or cord

nourishment: food that is necessary for life, health, and growth

oblong: longer than wide; rectangular; longer in one direction than in the other

obsidian: a hard shiny, usually dark-colored or black volcanic glass often used by the Indians to make arrowheads and knives

ochre: an earthy clay, colored by iron oxide, usually yellow or reddish brown and used to make paints

olivella: a type of sea snail with a bluish-purple shell about an inch long

ollas: jars or pots made of clay, used for holding water, seeds, etc.; storage vessels

oral histories: see oral tradition

oral tradition: history or background of a family, people, person, etc. passed on to others by the spoken word; stories, customs, past happenings told and passed on to others by speaking

paralyze: to make helpless or unable to move

pesticides: chemicals used for killing insects, weeds, etc.

pestle: a club-shaped hand tool made of stone for pounding seeds, acorns, herbs etc. into flour, meal, or pulp

petroglyphs: carvings done on a rock or rock wall, especially prehistoric carvings

physically: having to do with the body instead of the mind; rough play or activities

pictographs: symbols or pictures painted on rocks or rock walls, especially prehistoric picture-like symbols

pitch: a thick, sticky substance formed by certain evergreen trees; resin or sap of various trees

pithy: the soft, spongy tissue in the center of certain plant stems; a soft core

presidios: forts or military outposts

prey: an animal hunted or killed for food by another animal

productive: bringing forth, making, or creating goods, services, etc.; fertile

puck: a hard disk used by players of games such as shinny, hockey, etc.; a piece of wood or bone used as a ball in a game such as shinny

pump drill: see hand pump drill

quarries: places where building stone, marble, slate, etc. are dug out or excavated from the ground

radiocarbon: a small particle of carbon (a natural chemical element found in many substances) that gives off energy in the form of rays and helps tell or date the age of an ancient artifact, bone, rock, fossil, etc.

rancherias: small areas of land owned by Indians in California; a small ranch

ransacked: searched thoroughly and robbed

regalia: clothing made especially for special ceremonies, such as dance regalia

reinforced: given more strength; strengthened; made stronger

reservations: land granted to the Indians by the federal government of the United States

scorched: burned slightly to change the color, look, or texture of something; to char with intense heat

serpentine: a mineral or rock made mainly of magnesium silicate, green, yellow, brown in color and often streaked with red

silhouettes: outlines, dark shapes, or figures seen against a light background

sinew: the strong cord of tough fiber-like tissue that connects or attaches muscle to bones; a tendon

skim: to clear a liquid of floating matter; to remove floating matter from a liquid

slabs: pieces of wood, bark, etc. that are flat and thick; the rough outer pieces removed from a log or tree trunk

slingshots: Y-shaped sticks with leather straps attached to the prongs, used for shooting small stones

smallpox: a serious disease caused by a virus and easily spread with symptoms of fever, vomiting, and small red swellings or pimples that leave pitted scars or pockmarks when healed

snares: traps for small animals often using a loop of rope or cord that can be tighten when pulled

soggy: very wet; soaked; moist and heavy

spawn: to lay or produce eggs or young; the mass of eggs or young produced by fish, eels, toads, etc.

species: a group, kind, or variety of animals or plants having the same characteristics

spiritual: having to do with the soul or spirit of a person or thing; the thinking, feeling part of a person

spiritually: see spiritual

spokesperson: a person who speaks for another or for a group of people

stalking: walking or moving slowly and steadily toward game or an enemy

steatite: a soft stone for carving; a variety of talc; soapstone

substituted: put or used in place of another; to put instead of

sweathouse: a house built by the California Indians where a fire and red hot stones made the Indians sweat, used mainly by the men for sweating, fasting, smoking, games, initiations, dreaming, etc.

taikyuw: a sweathouse build by the Hupa Indians of Northern California

tanned: changing animal hides or skins into leather by soaking in a special liquid or solution

tannic acid: a yellowish, bitter substance made by the oak tree and found in acorns

tattoos: permanent marks or designs made on the skin with a needle

teasel: a plant that makes prickly cylinder-shaped seed pods used by the Indians for brushes

techniques: certain ways of doing or using something; special methods or manners of doing something

temporary: lasting for a time; not permanent

theory: an idea that is still being tested or explored and may not as yet be a proven fact

thongs: narrow strips of leather used for tying, binding, or strapping

throwing stick: a stick, often with a sharp point, that is thrown

tribal council: men and women elected by the adult members of the tribe to govern and help make decisions for the tribe

tripods: three-legged objects such as stools, tables, supports, etc.

tule: reed-like plants or bulrushes found near lakes or marshes having round, lightweight stems with pithy centers, used by the Indians for homes, boats, mats, sandals, etc.

tump line: a strap-like belt woven from plant fibers and worn across the forehead and over the shoulders to support a burden basket carried on the back

unique: being one of a kind; not like anyone or anything else

vagabonds: persons who move from place to place with no home; wanderers

vandals: persons who destroy public or private property, especially beautiful or artistic things; destructive people

vaqueros: a Spanish word for people who herd cattle, sheep, or horses; good horsemen

vast: very great in size, amount, or number; a very large space or area

vertebrae: the bones or segments of the spinal column

vertical: straight up; upright position

vibrations: movements back and forth; to move rapidly back and forth; to shake

watercraft: a boat or raft used on the water for carrying people or goods

watertight: so well put together that no water can get in or through; waterproof

wedges: pieces of wood, rock, or other hard materials that have a triangular shape with a thick end that narrows to a thin edge and is used for splitting wood, rocks, etc.

weirs: low dams or fence-like structures built in rivers or streams for catching fish

winatun: a special helper for some Yokuts chiefs whose duty was to greet all travelers, discuss their business, and, if necessary, take them to the chief

winnowing: blowing the husks or thin outer coverings from nuts and seeds by using a shallow basket to gently toss the seeds into the air and allowing the wind to blow away the skins, outer coverings, small particles, etc. that cannot be used

xonta: a family home built of wooden planks by the Hupa Indians of Northern California; a plank house

REFERENCE NOTES

Chapter One
Creation Stories of the California Indians
1. Bright, William. "Karok" in **Handbook of North American Indians, California**. Volume 8. Edited by Robert F. Heizer. Washington, D.C.: Smithsonian Institution, 1978, p. 187.
    Olmsted, D. L. and Stewart Omer C. "Achumawi" in **Handbook of North American Indians, California**, Volume 8. Edited by Robert F. Heizer. Washington, D.C.: Smithsonian Institution, 1978, p. 234.
    Wallace, William J. "Comparative Literature" in **Handbook of North American Indians, California**, Volume 8. Edited by Robert F. Heizer. Washington, D.C.: Smithsonian Institution, 1978, p. 658.
2. Bates, Craig. "The Maidu Story of Creation" in **News From Native California**. Volume 7, Number 1. Berkeley, California: Heyday Books, Winter-1992-1993, p 38.

A Scientific Story
3. Heizer, Robert F. "Introduction" in **Handbook of North American Indians, California**. Volume 8. Edited by Robert F. Heizer. Washington, D.C.: Smithsonian Institution, 1978, p. 3.
4. ————————.**The Great Geographical Atlas**. Chicago: Rand McNally Publishers, 1990, p. 194.
    ————————-. "Bering Strait" in **The World Book Encyclopedia**. Volume 2, B. Chicago: Field Enterprises Educational Corporation, 1965, p. 202.
    ————————-. "The First Americans" in **The World Book Encyclopedia**. Volume 10, I. Chicago: World Book, Inc., 1992, pp. 154-155.

Archeological Sites
5. Rector, Carol H. "Ancient Human and Animal Trackway" in **Archaeological Studies at Oro Grande Mojave Desert, California**. Assembled and edited By Carol H. Rector, Et al. Redlands, California: San Bernardino County Museum Association, 1983, pp. 161-164.
6. Rogers, Spencer L. **An Ancient Human Skeleton Found at Del Mar California**. San Diego Museum Papers No. 7. San Diego, California: San Diego Museum of Man, 1974.
    ————————-. "Archaeology" in **The World Book Encyclopedia**. Volume 1, A. Chicago: World Book, Inc., 1992, pp. 598-599.
    ————————-. "Radiocarbon" and "Radiocarbon Dating "in **The World Book Encyclopedia**. Volume 16, Q—R. Chicago: World Book, Inc., 1992, pp. 98-99.
    ————————-. "Geology" and "Geomorphology" in **The World Book Encyclopedia**. Volume 8, G. Chicago: World Book, Inc., 1992, pp. 100-101, 107.
7. Heizer, Robert F., p. 3. ————————————

Chapter Two
California's First Inhabitants
1. Sherburne, Cook F. "Historical Demography" in **Handbook of North American Indians, California**. Volume 8. Edited by Robert F. Heizer. Washington, D.C. : Smithsonian Institution, 1978,p. 91.
2. Shipley, William F. "Native Languages of California" in **Handbook of North American Indians, California**. Volume 8. Edited by Robert F. Heizer. Washington, D.C.: Smithsonian Institution, 1978, p. 80.
3. Mc Lendon, Sally and Oswalt, Robert L. "Pomo: Introduction" in **Handbook of North American Indians, California**. Volume 8. Edited by Robert F. Heizer. Washington, D.C.: Smithsonian Institution, 1978, p. 283.

Women's Belongings and Tools
4. Kelly, Isabel. "Coast Miwok" in **Handbook of North American Indians, California**. Volume 8. Edited by Robert F. Heizer. Washington, D.C.: Smithsonian Institution, 1978, p. 419.
5. Kroeber, A. L. **Handbook of the Indians of California**. Bulletin 78, Smithsonian Institution, Bureau of American Ethnology. Washington, D. C.: Government Printing Office, 1925, pp. 446-447.
6. Kroeber, A. L., pp. 827—828.
    Latta, Frank F. **Handbook of Yokuts Indians**. Santa Cruz, California: Bear State Books, 1977, p. 540.
7. Brown, Vinson and Andrews, Douglas. **The Pomo Indians of California and Their Neighbors**. Healdsburg, California: Naturegraph Publishers, 1969,p 32.
    James, Harry C. **The Cahuilla Indians**. Morongo Indian Reservation: Malki Museum Press, 1985, p. 55.
    Powers, Stephen. **Tribes of California**. Berkeley, California: University of California Press, 1976, p. 47.
    Heizer, Robert F. and Treganza A. E. "Mines and Quarries of the Indians of California" in **The California Indians, a Sourcebook**. Compiled and edited by R. F. Heizer and M. A. Whipple. Berkeley, California: University of California Press, 1973, p. 354.
8. Kroeber, A.L., pp.807-808.
    James, Harry C., p.55
    Potts, Marie. **The Northern Maidu**. Happy Camp, California: Naturegraph Publishers, Inc., 1977,p. 24
    Nelson, Byron. **Our Home Forever, A Hupa Tribal History**. Hoopa, California: Hupa Tribe, 1978, pp.7,22,141.
9. Kroeber, A. L. , pp. 591, 698, 827—828.

Men's Belongings and Tools

10. Brown, Vinson and Andrews, Douglas, pp. 24, 26—27.
    Riddell, Francis A. "Maidu and Konkow" in **Handbook of North American Indians, California**. Volume 8. Edited by Robert F. Heizer. Washington, D.C.: Smithsonian Institution, 1978, p. 383.
    Kroeber, A. L., pp. 86, 326, 361-362, 805-806, 815-816.
11. Kroeber, A.L., pp. 90-plate 19, 94, 287.
    Elsasser, Albert B. "Development of Regional Prehistoric Cultures" in **Handbook of North American Indians, California**. Volume 8. Edited by Robert F. Heizer. Washington, D.C.: Smithsonian Institution, 1978, p. 51.
    Bright, William. "Karok" in **Handbook of North American Indians, California**. Volume 8. Edited by Robert F. Heizer. Washington, D.C.: Smithsonian Institution, 1978, p. 183.
12. Brown, Vinson and Andrews, Douglas, p. 27.
    Kroeber, A.L., pp. 90-plate 16, 332, 530.

Bows and Arrows

13. Brown, Vinson and Andrews, Douglas, p.21.
    Kroeber, A.L., pp. 417, 817-818.

Chapter Three

Trade Among The Indians

1. Miller, Bruce W. **Chumash, A Picture of Their World**. Los Osos, California: Sand River Press, 1988, p 111.
   Garth, T.R. "Atsugewi" in **Handbook of North American Indians, California**. Volume 8. Edited by Robert F. Heizer. Washington, D.C.: Smithsonian Institution, 1978, p. 239.
2. Heizer, Robert F. "Trade and Trails" in **Handbook of North American Indians, California**. Volume 8. Edited by Robert F. Heizer. Washington, D.C.: Smithsonian Institution, 1978, p. 690.
3. Kroeber, A. L. **Handbook of the Indians of California**. Bulletin 78, Smithsonian Institution, Bureau of American Ethnology. Washington, D.C.: Government Printing Office, 1925, p. 132.
   Nelson, Byron. **Our Home Forever, A Hupa Tribal History**. Hoopa, California: Hupa Tribe, 1978, p. 18.
4. Goldschmidt, Walter, et al. "War Stories From Two Enemy Tribes" in **The California Indians, a Sourcebook**. Compiled and edited by R. F. Heizer and M. A. Whipple. Berkeley, California: University of California Press, 1973, p. 447.
5. Beardsley, Richard K. "Culture Sequences in Central California Archaeology " **The California Indians, A Sourcebook**. Compiled and edited by R. F. Heizer and M.A. Whipple. Berkeley, California: University of California Press, 1973, p. 181.
6. Heizer, R. F. and Treganza, A.E. "Mines and Quarries of the Indians of California" **The California Indians, A Sourcebook**. Compiled and edited by R. F. Heizer and M.A. Whipple. Berkeley, California: University of California Press, 1973, p. 354.
7. Bean, Lowell John and Smith, Charles R. "Gabrielino" in **Handbook of North American Indians, California**. Volume 8. Edited by Robert F. Heizer. Washington, D.C.: Smithsonian Institution, 1978, p.547.
8. Bean, Lowell John and Smith, Charles R. "Gabrielino" in **Handbook of North American Indians, California**. Volume 8. Edited by Robert F. Heizer. Washington, D.C.: Smithsonian Institution, 1978, p. 547.
   Bean, Lowell John. "Cahuilla" in **Handbook of North American Indians, California** Volume 8. Edited by Robert F. Heizer. Washington, D.C.: Smithsonian Institution, 1978, p. 582.
9. Heizer, Robert F., p. 690-693.
10. Goldschmidt, Walter. "Nomlaki" **Handbook of North American Indians, California**. Volume 8. Edited by Robert F. Heizer. Washington, D.C.: Smithsonian Institution, 1978, p. 345.
    Heizer R. F. and Treganza A.E., p. 353.
    Miller, Bruce W., p. 112.

Trade Money

11. Elsasser, Albert B. "Development of Regional Prehistoric Cultures" in **Handbook of North American Indians, California**. Volume 8. Edited by Robert F. Heizer. Washington, D.C.: Smithsonian Institution, 1978, p. 51.
    Wallace, William J. "Hupa, Chilula, and Whilkut" in **Handbook of North American Indians, California**. Volume 8. Edited by Robert F. Heizer. Washington, D.C.: Smithsonian Institution, 1978, pp. 168-169.
    Mc Lendon, Sally and Lowy, Michael J. "Eastern Pomo and Southeastern Pomo" in **Handbook of North American Indians, California**. Volume 8. Edited by Robert F. Heizer. Washington, D.C.: Smithsonian Institution, 1978, p. 314.
    Riddell, Francis A. "Maidu and Konkow" in **Handbook of North American Indians, California**. Volume 8. Edited by Robert F. Heizer. Washington, D.C.: Smithsonian Institution, 1978, p. 380.
    Kroeber, A.L., p. 22-23, 824-825.

Clamshell Beads

12. King, Chester. "Protohistoric and Historic Archeology" in **Handbook of North American Indians, California**. Volume 8. Edited by Robert F. Heizer. Washington, D.C.: Smithsonian Institution, 1978, pp. 61-62.
13. Bean, Lowell John and Smith, Charles R. "Gabrielino" in **Handbook of North American Indians, California**. Volume 8. Edited by Robert F. Heizer. Washington, D.C.: Smithsonian Institution, 1978, p. 547.
    Heizer, Robert F., p. 691.
14. Kroeber, A.L., pp. 176, 421.
    Riddell, Francis A., p. 380.

15. King, Chester, p.61.
16. Kroeber, A.L., pp. 248,825.
17. Kroeber, A.L.,pp. 564,825.
18. Kroeber, A.L. pp. 248-249, 421.
19. King, Chester, p. 61.

Dentalium Shells

20. Kroeber, A.L., p. 22.
    Elsasser, Albert B., p. 51.
21. Kroeber, A.L., p. 25.
22. Kroeber, A.L., pp. 22-25, 78-plate 11.
    Nelson, Byron, p. 18.
    Wallace, William J., p. 168.
23. Powers, Stephen. **Tribes of California**. Berkeley, California: University of California Press, 1976, p. 76.
24. Wallace, William J., p. 168.
    Kroeber, A.L., p. 24.
25. Elsasser, Albert B., p.51.

Magnesite

26. Kroeber, A.L., p. 176.
27 Kroeber, A.L., pp. 249,825.

Trade Routes

28. Heizer, Robert. F.,pp. 690-693.

Chapter Four

The Mighty Oak

1. Pavlik, Bruce M., et al. **Oaks of California**. Los Olivos, California: Cachuma Press, Inc., 1992, p.3.
2. Pavlik, Bruce M., et al., p. 36.

Gathering Acorns

3. Alvarez, Susan H. and Peri, David W. "Acorns: The Staff of Life" in **News From Native California.** Volume 1, Number 4. Berkeley, California: Heyday Book, September/November, 1987, pp. 10-14.
4. Pavlik, Bruce M., et al., p. 97.
    Lawson, Vana., Nursery Assistant, Ya-Ka-Ama Indian Education and Development Inc., Forestville, California, 1993.
5. Garth, T. R. "Atsugewi" in **Handbook of North American Indians, California**. Volume 8. Edited by Robert F. Heizer. Washington, D.C.: Smithsonian Institution, 1978, p. 243.
    Myers, James E. "Cahto" in **Handbook of North American Indians, California**. Volume 8. Edited by Robert F. Heizer. Washington, D.C.: Smithsonian Institution, p. 246.
6. Pavlik, Bruce. M., et al., p. 98.
7. Alvarez, Susan H. and Peri, David W., pp. 10-14
    Pavlik, Bruce M., et al., p. 98.
8. Pavlik, Bruce M., et al., p. 98.
9. Alvarez, Susan H. and Peri, David W., pp.10-14
    Gould, Richard A. "Tolowa" in **Handbook of North American Indians, California**. Volume 8. Edited by Robert F. Heizer. Washington, D.C.: Smithsonian Institution, 1978, p. 128.
    Pilling, Arnold R. "Yurok" in **Handbook of North American Indians, California**. Volume 8. Edited by Robert F. Heizer. Washington, D.C.: Smithsonian Institution, 1978, p. 146.
    Lawson, Vana. Nursery Assistant. Ya-Ka-Ama Indian Education and Development Inc., Forestville, California, 1993.
10. Garth, T. R., p. 238.

Storing Acorns

11. Kroeber, A. L. in **Handbook of the Indians of California**. Bulletin 78, Smithsonian Institution, Bureau of American Ethnology. Washington, D.C.: Government Printing Office, 1925, pp. 446-447, 828-829.
    Levy, Richard. "Eastern Miwok" in **Handbook of North American Indians, California**. Volume 8. Edited by Robert F. Heizer. Washington, D.C.: Smithsonian Institution, 1978, p. 409.
    Pavlik, Bruce M., et al., pp. 98-99.
    Heizer, Robert F. and Elsasser, Albert B. **The Natural World of the California Indians**. Berkeley, California: University of California Press, 1980, pp. 94,99.
    Barrett, S.A. and Gifford E.W. "Miwok Houses" in **The California Indians, A Sourcebook**. Compiled and edited by R.F. Heizer and M.A. Whipple. Berkeley, California: University of California Press, 1973, pp.339-340.
    Powers, Stephen. **Tribes of California**. Berkeley, California: University of California Press, 1976, P. 284.
    Potts, Marie. **The Northern Maidu**. Happy Camp, California: Naturegraph Publishers, Inc., 1977,p 14.
    Alvarez, Susan H. and Peri, David W., pp. 10-14.

Preparing Acorns

12. Alvarez, Susan H. and Peri, David W., pp. 10-14.
    Heizer, Robert F. and Elsasser, Albert B., p. 93.

Kroeber, A. L., pp. 88, 293, 446, 467, 527, 814.

Knudtson, Peter M. **The Wintun Indians of California and Their Neighbors**. Happy Camp, California: Naturegraph Publishers, Inc., 1977,p. 39.

Brown, Vinson and Andrews, Douglas. **The Pomo Indians of California and Their Neighbors**. Healdsburg, California: Naturegraph Publishers, 1969, p. 15.

Pavlik, Bruce M., et al.,pp. 98-101.

Cooking With Acorns Today

13. Peri, David W. "Cooking with Acorns" in **News From Native California**. Volume 1, Number 4. Berkeley, California: Heyday Books, September/November, 1987, p. 22.

Pavlik, Bruce M., et al., pp. 100-101, 116-117.

Ortiz, Bev. **It will Live Forever-Traditional Yosemite Indian Acorn Preparation**.Berkeley, California: Heyday Books, 1991, pp. 147-148.

Supahan, Sarah, Editor. **Indians of Northwest California, A History/Social Science Literature Based Curriculum Unit**. Hoopa, California: Klamath—Trinity Joint Unified School Districts, 1992, pp. 81-82, 88.

Agave

14. Bean, Lowell John and Saubel, Katherine Siva. **Temalpakh, Cahuilla Indian Knowledge and Useage of Plants**. Banning, California: Malki Museum Press, 1972, pp. 31-36

Balls, Edward K. Early Uses of California Plants. Berkeley, California: University of California Press, 1975, pp. 17-20.

Clarke, Charlotte B. **Edible and Useful Plants of California**. Berkeley, California: University of California Press, 1977, pp. 99-101.

Mesquite

15. Bean, Lowell John and Saubel, Katherine Siva, pp.107-118.

Balls, Edward K., pp. 20-21.

Clarke, Charlotte B., pp. 123-125.

James, Harry C. **The Cahuilla Indians**. Morongo Indian Reservation: Malki Museum Press, 1985, p. 55.

Pinenuts

16. Bean, Lowell John and Saubel, Katherine Siva, pp.102-105.

Wheat, Margaret M. **Survival Arts of the Primitive Paiutes**. Reno, Nevada: University of Nevada Press, 1967, pp. 29-39.

Balls, Edward K., pp. 28-29.

Sweet, Muriel. **Common Edible and Useful Plants of the West**. Happy Camp, California: Naturegraph Publishers, Inc., 1976, p. 14.

Miller, Kit. "Pinenuts" in **Native Peoples Magazine**. Volume 5, Number 4. Phoenix, Arizona: Media Concepts Group, Inc., Summer, 1992, pp. 48-52.

Some Indians Planted Crops

17. Kroeber, A.L., p. 735.

Bright, William. "Karok" in **Handbook of North American Indians, California**. Volume 8. Edited by Robert F. Heizer. Washington, D.C.: Smithsonian Institution, 1978, p. 183.

Silver, Shirley. "Shastan Peoples" in **Handbook of North American Indians, California**. Volume 8. Edited by Robert F. Heizer. Washington, D.C.: Smithsonian Institution, 1978, p. 222.

Other Native Plants Used By The Indians

18. Powers, Stephen., pp. 86,424-425,429. Andreoli, Andrew. Director of Indian Teacher Education Personnel Program, Humboldt State University, 1993.

Lawson, Vana. Nursery Assistant. Ya-Ka-Ama Indian Education and Development Inc., Forestville, California, 1993.

19. Balls, Edward K., pp.. 31-32.

Clarke, Charlotte B., pp. 140-141.

20. Balls, Edward K., pp.34-35.

Clarke, Charlotte B., pp. 102-106.

21. Balls, Edward K., pp. 41-42.

Clarke, Charlotte B., pp. 46-47.

22. Balls, Edward K., pp. 46-47.

23. Clarke, Charlotte B., pp.26-27.

24. Balls, Edward K., pp. 15-17.

Clarke, Charlotte B., pp. 19-20.

25. Clarke,Charlotte B., pp. 23-24.

26. Balls, Edward K., p. 31.

Clarke, Charlotte B., pp. 30-31.

Sweet, Muriel., pp. 198,243.

27. Balls, Edward K., pp. 90-91.

Nyerges, Christopher. **A Southern Californian's Guide to Wild Food**. Los Angeles, California: Christopher Nyerges and Janice Fryling, 1980, p. 48.

28. Balls, Edward K., pp. 32-33, 90.

Clarke, Charlotte B., pp. 144.

29. Sweet, Muriel., p. 19.

30. Balls, Edward K., p. 25.
   Clarke, Charlotte B., pp. 110-112.
   Sweet, Muriel., pp. 36.

31. Balls, Edward K., p. 91.
   Clarke, Charlotte B., pp. 114-115.

32. Clarke, Charlotte B., pp. 39-41.
   Niethammer, Carolyn. **American Indian Food and Lore**. New York, New York: Macmillan Publishing Co., Inc., 1978, pp.63-67.
   Nyerges, Christopher. , pp. 62-63.

33. Balls, Edward K., p. 91.
   Sweet, Muriel., p. 23.

34. Balls, Edward K., pp. 80-81.
   Clarke, Charlotte B., p. 165.

35. Balls, Edward., pp.57-58, 79-80.

36. Balls, Edward K., pp.71-72.
   Sweet, Muriel., p. 47.

37. Balls, Edward K., pp. 66-67.
   Bean, Lowell John and Saubel, Katherine Siva., pp. 60-65.
   Kroeber, A.L., pp. 502-505.

38. Balls, Edward K., pp. 38-39.
   Clarke, Charlotte B., pp. 55-56.

39. Balls, Edward K., p. 78-79.
   Clarke, Charlotte B., pp. 57-58

40. Nyerges, Christopher., pp. 102-103.
   Powers, Stephen., p. 425.
   Clarke, Charlotte B., pp. 59-60.

41. Clarke, Charlotte B., pp. 160-161.
   Collins, Margit Roos. **The Flavors of Home**. Berkeley, California: Heyday Books, 1990, pp. 120-121.
   Sweet, Muriel., p.53.
   Lawson, Vana. Nursery Assistant. Ya-Ka-Ama Indian Education and Development Inc., Forestville, California, 1993.

42. Clarke, Charlotte B., pp. 155-156.

43. Clarke, Charlotte B., pp. 47-49.
   Niethammer, Carolyn., pp. 68-69.

44. Balls,Edward., pp. 58-59.

45. Clarke, Charlotte B., pp. 69-71
   Nyerges, Christopher., p. 29.
   Niethammer, Carolyn., pp. 98-99.

46. Clarke, Charlotte B., pp. 88-82.
   Niethammer, Carolyn., pp.77-78.
   Sweet, Muriel., p. 29.

47. Balls, Edward K., pp. 81-82
   Bean, Lowell John and Saubel, Katherine Siva., pp. 90-94.

48. Eliot, Willard A. **Forest Trees of the Pacific Coast**. New York, New York: Van Rees Press, 1948, pp. 316-479.

49. Balls, Edward K., pp. 63-64.
   Clarke, Charlotte B., pp. 226-227.
   Sweet, Muriel., p. 30.

50. Balls, Edward K., pp. 44-45.
   Nyerges, Christopher., p.197.

Chapter Five

Hunting and Fishing

1. Olmsted, D.L. and Stewart, Omer C. "Achumawi" in **Handbook of North American Indians, California**. Volume 8. Edited by Robert F. Heizer. Washington, D.C.: Smithsonian Institution, 1978, p. 225.

2. Bright, William. "Karok" in **Handbook of North American Indians, California**. Volume 8. Edited by Robert F. Heizer. Washington, D.C.: Smithsonian Institution, 1978, p. 181.
   Garth, T.R. "Atsugewi" in **Handbook of North American Indians, California**. Volume 8. Edited by Robert F. Heizer. Washington, D.C.: Smithsonian Institution, 1978, p. 243.

3. Elsasser, Albert B. "Development of Regional Prehistoric Cultures" in **Handbook of North American Indians, California**. Volume 8. Edited by Robert F. Heizer. Washington, D.C.: Smithsonian Institution, 1978, p. 46.
   Silver, Shirley. "Shastan Peoples" in **Handbook of North American Indians, California**. Volume 8. Edited by Robert F.

Heizer. Washington, D.C.: Smithsonian Institution, 1978, p. 216.

Kelly, Isabel. "Coast Miwok" in **Handbook of North American Indians, California**. Volume 8. Edited by Robert F. Heizer. Washington, D.C.: Smithsonian Institution, 1978, p. 416.

Kroeber, A.L., **Handbook of the Indians of California**. Bulletin 78, Smithsonian Institution, Bureau of American Ethnology. Washington, D.C.: Government Printing Office, 1925, pp. 174, 410.

4.   Garth, T. R., p. 242

Miller, Virginia P. "Yuki Huchnom, and Coast Yuki" in **Handbook of North American Indians, California**. Volume 8. Edited by Robert F. Heizer. Washington, D.C.: Smithsonian Institution, 1978, p. 252.

Kroeber, A.L., p. 526.

5.   Wallace, William J. "Southern Valley Yokuts" in **Handbook of North American Indians, California**. Volume 8. Edited by Robert F. Heizer. Washington, D.C.: Smithsonian Institution, 1978, p. 450.

6.   Garth, T. R., p. 238.

Deer Hunting

7.   Kroeber, A.L., pp. 295,528,817.

Silver, Shirley, p. 216.

Brown, Vinson and Andrews, Douglas. **The Pomo Indians of California and Their Neighbors**. Healdsburg, California: Naturegraph Publishers, 1969, p. 18.

Latta, Frank F. **Handbook of Yokuts Indians**. Santa Cruz, California: Bear State Books, 1977,p. 497.

Excellent Ecologists

8.   Nelson, Byron. **Our Home Forever, A Hupa Tribal History**.Hoopa, California: Hupa Tribe, 1978, p. 16.

Andreoli, Andrew. Director of Indian Teacher Education Personnel Program, Humboldt State University, 1993.

Hunting Small Game

9.   Kroeber, A.L., pp. 632,652.

10. Brown, Vinson and Andrews, Douglas, p. 20.

11. Brown, Vinson and Andrews, Douglas, p. 20.

12. Kroeber, A.L., pp. 531, 845.

Fishing

13. Brown, Vinson and Andrews, Douglas, p. 22.

Miller, Bruce W. **Chumash, A Picture of Their World**. Los Osos, California: Sand River Press, 1988, p. 84.

Kroeber, A.L., pp. 326,815.

14. Kroeber, A.L., p. 816.

15. Nelson,Byron, pp. 25-30.

Wallace, William J. "Hupa, Chilula, and Whilkut" in **Handbook of North American Indians, California**. Volume 8. Edited by Robert F. Heizer. Washington, D.C.: Smithsonian Institution, 1978, p. 165.

16. Kroeber, A.L., p. 172, plate 33.

17. Kroeber, A.L., pp. 86,815-816.

Brown, Vinson and Andrews, Douglas, p. 22.

18. Kroeber, A.L., pp. 528-529, 816-817.

Wallace, William J., p. 165.

19. Schulz, Paul. **The Indians of Lassen Volcanic National Park and Vicinity**. Mineral, California: Loomis Museum Association, 1954, pp. 46-47.

Kroeber, A. L., p. 294.

Mauldin, Henry K. **History of Clear Lake, Mt. Konocti and the Lake County Cattle Industry**. Kelseyville, California: Anderson Printing, 1968, pp. 6-7.

Salmon and Lamprey Eels

20. Kroeber, A.L., p. 294.

Gould, Richard A. "Tolowa" in **Handbook of North American Indians, California**. Volume 8. Edited by Robert F. Heizer. Washington, D.C.: Smithsonian Institution, 1978, p. 134.

Pilling, Arnold R. "Yurok" in **Handbook of North American Indians, California**. Volume 8. Edited by Robert F. Heizer. Washington, D.C.: Smithsonian Institution, 1978, p. 148.

Wallace, William J., p. 174.

Bright, William, p. 181.

Nelson, Byron, pp. 28-29.

Heizer, Robert F. and Elsasser, Albert B. **The Natural World of the California Indians**. Berkeley, California: University of California Press, 1980, p. 211.

Thompson, Lucy. **To the American Indian, Reminiscences of a Yurok Woman**. Berkeley, California: Heyday Books, 1991, pp. 177-180, 196.

Grzimek, Bernhard. Editor-in-Chief. **Grzimek's Animal Life Encyclopedia**. New York, New York: Van Nostrand Reinhold Company, 1973, pp. 34-37.

Food From The Sea
21. Heizer, Robert F. and Elsasser, Albert B., p. 62.

   Grant, Campbell. "Eastern Coastal Chumash" in **Handbook of North American Indians, California**. Volume 8. Edited by Robert F. Heizer. Washington, D.C.: Smithsonian Institution, 1978, p. 517.

   Kroeber, A.L., pp. 919-932.

22. Gould, Richard A., p. 134.

   Kroeber, A.L., pp. 86,816.

   Heizer, Robert F. and Elsasser, Albert B., pp. 156,162-164.

Whales
23. Heizer, Robert F. and Elsasser, Albert B., p. 119

   Kroeber, A.L., p.467.

   Levy, Richard. "Costanoan" in **Handbook of North American Indians, California**. Volume 8. Edited by Robert F. Heizer. Washington, D.C.: Smithsonian Institution, 1978, p. 491.

   Grant, Campbell, pp. 511,517.

Sea Birds
24. Margolin, Malcolm. **The Ohlone Way, Indian Life in the San Francisco—Monterey Bay Area**. Berkeley, California: Heyday Books, 1978, pp, 37-38.

Chapter Six
Basketmaking
1. Mc Call, Lynne and Perry, Rosalind, et al. **The Chumash People, Materials for Teachers and Students**. Santa Barbara, California: Santa Barbara Museum of Natural History, 1982, pp. 85-87.

2. Heizer, Robert F. and Elsasser, Albert B. **The Natural World of the California Indians**. Berkeley California: University of California Press, 1980, p. 132.

   Ortiz, Bev with the staff from **News From Native California. California Indian Basketweavers Gathering, June 28-30, 1991, A Special Report**. Berkeley, California: Heyday Books, Winter, 1991-92.

Twined and Coiled Baskets
3. Kroeber, A. L. "California Basketry and the Pomo" in **The California Indians, A Sourcebook**. Compiled and edited by Robert F. Heizer and M. A. Whipple. Berkeley, California: University of California Press, 1973, p.321.

4. Gould, Richard A. "Tolowa" in **Handbook of North American Indians, California**. Volume 8. Edited by Robert F. Heizer. Washington, D.C.: Smithsonian Institution, 1978, p. 129.

   Wallace, William J. "Hupa, Chilula, and Whilkut" in **Handbook of North American Indians, California**. Volume 8. Edited by Robert F. Heizer. Washington, D.C.: Smithsonian Institution, 1978, p. 167.

   Elsasser, Albert B. "Basketry" in **Handbook of North American Indians, California**. Volume 8. Edited by Robert F. Heizer. Washington, D.C.: Smithsonian Institution, 1978, p. 626.

   Kroeber, A. L. **Handbook of the Indians of California**. Bulletin 78, Smithsonian Institution, Bureau of American Ethnology. Washington, D.C.: Government Printing Office, 1925, pp. 531-534, 591, 819-822.

   Kroeber, A. L. "California Basketry and The Pomo", pp. 320-321, 331.

   Latta, Frank F. **Handbook of Yokuts Indians**. Santa Cruz, California: Bear State Books, 1977, pp.533-537.

   Brown, Vinson and Andrews, Douglas, **The Pomo Indians of California and Their Neighbors**. Healdsburg, California: Naturegraph Publishers, 1969, p. 36.

5. Kroeber, A. L. "California Basketry and The Pomo", p. 331.

   Beard, Yolande S. **The Wappo—A Report**. Banning, California: Malki Museum Press, 1979, p. 58.

Basket Materials of the Northern California Indians
6. Powers, Stephen. **Tribes of California**. Berkeley, California: University of California Press, 1976, p. 377.

   Heizer, Robert F. and Elsasser, Albert B., p. 136.

   Kroeber, A. L. **Handbook of the Indians of California**, pp. 819-829.

   Wallace, William J., p. 167.

   Bright, William. "Karok" in **Handbook of North American Indians, California.** Volume 8. Edited by Robert F. Heizer. Washington, D.C.: Smithsonian Institution, 1978, p. 183.

Basket Materials of the Southern California Indians
7. Farmer, Justin F. "Basketry of the Southern California 'Mission' Indians" in News From Native California. Volume 2, Number 1. Berkeley, California: Heyday Books, March/April, 1988, pp. 8-10.

   Mc Call, Lynne and Perry, Rosalind, et al., p. 87.

   Kroeber, A. L. Handbook of the Indians of California, pp. 698-699, 820.

   Kroeber, A. L. "California Basketry and the Pomo", p. 331.

Waterproof Basketry
8. Elsasser, Albert B. "Basketry", pp. 634-635.

   Mc Call, Lynne and Perry, Rosalind., p. 88.

   Kroeber, A. L. **Handbook of the Indians of California**, pp. 561, 571.

Bottomless Pounding Baskets
9.   Elsasser, Albert B. "Basketry", p. 634.

Decorated Baskets
10.   Kroeber, A. L. **Handbook of the Indians of California**, pp. 244-249.
      Kroeber A. L. "California Basketry and The Pomo", pp. 322, 331.
      Callaghan, Catherine A. "Lake Miwok" in **Handbook of North American Indians, California**. Volume 8. Edited by Robert F. Heizer. Washington, D.C.: Smithsonian Institution, 1978, p. 266.
      Elsasser, Albert B. "Basketry", p. 626.
      Brown, Vinson and Andrews, Douglas., pp. 34-36.

Bowls
11.   Kroeber, A. L. **Handbook of the Indians of California**, pp. 737-738, 822-823.
      Luomala, Katharine. "Tipai-Ipai" in **Handbook of North American Indians, California**. Volume 8. Edited by Robert F. Heizer. Washington, D.C.: Smithsonian Institution, 1978, p. 600.
12.   Kroeber, A. L. **Handbook of the Indians of California**, p. 337.
      Clements, Lydia. **The Indians of Death Valley**. Hollywood, California: Cloister Press of Hollywood, 1975, p. 13.
13.   Kroeber, A. L. **Handbook of the Indians of California**, pp. 562, 629-630.
      Elsasser, Albert B. "Development of Regional Prehistoric Cultures" in **Handbook of North American Indians, California**. Volume 8. Edited by Robert F. Heizer. Washington, D.C.: Smithsonian Institution, 1978, p. 54.
      King, Chester. "Protohistoric and Historic Archeology" in **Handbook of North American Indians, California**. Volume 8. Edited by Robert F. Heizer. Washington, D.C.: Smithsonian Institution, 1978, p. 62.
      Bright, William., p. 183.
      Silver, Shirley. "Chimariko" in **Handbook of North American Indians, California**. Volume 8. Edited by Robert F. Heizer. Washington, D.C.: Smithsonian Institution, 1978, p. 207.
      Silver, Shirley. "Shastan Peoples" in **Handbook of North American Indians, California**. Volume 8. Edited by Robert F. Heizer. Washington, D.C.: Smithsonian Institution, 1978, p. 218.
      Wilson, Norman L. and Towne, Arlean H. "Nisenan" in **Handbook of North American Indians, California**. Volume 8. Edited by Robert F. Heizer. Washington, D.C.: Smithsonian Institution, 1978, p. 391.
      Hester, Thomas Roy. "Salinan" in **Handbook of North American Indians, California**. Volume 8. Edited by Robert F. Heizer. Washington, D.C.: Smithsonian Institution, 1978, p. 501.
      Grant, Campbell., "Eastern Coastal Chumash" in **Handbook of North American Indians, California**. Volume 8. Edited by Robert F. Heizer. Washington, D.C.: Smithsonian Institution, 1978, pp. 514-515, 517.
14.   Grant, Campbell., p. 516.

Boats
15.   Kroeber, A. L. **Handbook of the Indians of California**, p. 813.
      Elsasser, Albert B. "Mattole, Nongatl, Sinkyone, Lassik, and Wailaki" in **Handbook of North American Indians, California**. Volume 8. Edited by Robert F. Heizer. Washington, D.C.: Smithsonian Institution, 1978, p. 201.

Tule Boats
16.   Wheat, Margaret M. **Survival Arts of the Primitive Paiutes**. Reno, Nevada: University of Nevada Press, 1967, pp. 40, 46-47.
      Latta, Frank F., p. 503.
      Schulz, Paul E. **Indians of Lassen Volcanic National Park and Vicinity**. Mineral, California: Loomis Museum Association, Lassen Volcanic National Park, 1954, pp. 100-101.
      Kroeber, A. L. **Handbook of the Indians of California**, pp. 243, 813-814.
      Brown, Vinson and Andrews, Douglas., p. 28.
      Margolin, Malcolm. **The Ohlone Way Indian Life in the San Francisco—Monterey Bay Area**. Berkeley, California: Heyday Books, 1978, pp. 37-38.

Dug-out Canoes
17.   Kroeber, A. L. **Handbook of the Indians of California**, pp. 82-83.
      Powers, Stephen., p. 69.
      Gould, Richard A., p. 130.
      Elsasser, Albert B. "Mattole, Nongatl, Sinkyone, Lassik, and Wailaki", p. 201.
      Silver, Shirley. "Chimariko", p. 208.
      Silver, Shirley. "Shastan Peoples", p. 218.
      Olmsted, D. L. and Stewart, Omer C. "Achumawi" in **Handbook of North American Indians, California**. Volume 8. Edited by Robert F. Heizer. Washington, D.C.: Smithsonian Institution, 1978, p. 229.
      Wilson, Norman L. and Towne, Arlean H., p. 389.
      Margolin, Malcolm. "California Watercraft: Ongoing Traditions" in **News From Native California**. Volume 2, Number 4. Berkeley, California: Heyday Books, September/October, 1988, pp. 14-19.

Plank Boats
18.   McCall, Lynne and Perry, Rosalind, et al., pp. 41-43.
      Kroeber, A.L. Handbook of the Indians of California, pp. 558-559, 630, 813.
      Margolin, Malcolm. "California Watercrafts: Ongoing Traditions", pp. 16-18.

Chapter Seven
Everyday Wear
1. Kroeber, A.L., in **Handbook of the Indians of California**. Bulletin 78, Smithsonian Institution, Bureau of American Ethnology. Washington, D.C.: Government Printing Office, 1925, pp. 76, 173, 240, 276, 721, 804.

    Elsasser, Albert B. "Wiyot" in **Handbook of North American Indians, California**. Volume 8. Edited by Robert F. Heizer. Washington, D.C.: Smithsonian Institution, 1978, p. 158.

    Wallace, William J. "Hupa, Chilula, and Whilkut" in **Handbook of North American Indians, California**. Volume 8. Edited by Robert F. Heizer. Washington, D.C.: Smithsonian Institution, 1978, p. 167.

    Bright, William. "Karok" in **Handbook of North American Indians, California**. Volume 8. Edited by Robert F. Heizer. Washington, D.C.: Smithsonian Institution, 1978, p. 184.

    Elsasser, Albert B. "Mattole, Nongatl, Sinkyone, Lassik, and Wailaki" in **Handbook of North American Indians, California**. Volume 8. Edited by Robert F. Heizer. Washington, D.C.: Smithsonian Institution, 1978, p. 202.

    Bean, Lowell John and Theodoratus, Dorothea. "Western Pomo and Northeastern Pomo" in **Handbook of North American Indians, California**. Volume 8. Edited by Robert F. Heizer. Washington, D.C.: Smithsonian Institution, 1978, p. 291.

    La Pena, Frank R. "Wintu" in **Handbook of North American Indians, California**. Volume 8. Edited by Robert F. Heizer. Washington, D.C.: Smithsonian Institution, 1978, p. 335.

    Bean, Lowell John and Smith, Charles R. "Gabrielino" in **Handbook of North American Indians, California**. Volume 8. Edited by Robert F. Heizer. Washington, D.C.: Smithsonian Institution, 1978, p. 541.

    Bean, Lowell John and Shipek, Florence C. "Luiseno" in **Handbook of North American Indians, California**. Volume 8. Edited by Robert F. Heizer. Washington, D.C.: Smithsonian Institution, 1978, p. 554.

    Luomala, Katharine. "Tipai—Ipai" in **Handbook of North American Indians, California**. Volume 8. Edited by Robert F. Heizer. Washington, D.C.: Smithsonian Institution, 1978, p. 599.

    Wheat, Margaret M. **Survival Arts of the Primitive Paiutes**. Reno, Nevada: University of Nevada Press, 1967, p. 75.

Colder Days
2. Kroeber, A.L., pp. 76, 173, 276,416, 467,562, 804-805.

    Elsasser, Albert B. "Wiyot", p. 159.

    Wallace, William J., p. 167.

    Elsasser, Albert B. "Mattole, Nongatl, Sinkyone, Lassik, and Wailaki", p. 202.

    Bean, Lowell John and Theodoratus, Dorothea., p. 291.

    Wilson, Norman L. and Towne, Arlean H. "Nisenan" in **Handbook of North American Indians, California**. Volume 8. Edited by Robert F. Heizer. Washington, D.C.: Smithsonian Institution, 1978, pp. 389, 391.

    Bean, Lowell John and Smith, Charles R., p. 541.

    Bean, Lowell John and Shipek, Florence C., p. 554.

    Luomala, Katherine., p. 599.

    Wheat, Margaret M., pp. 74-77.

    Brusa, Betty War. **Salinan Indians of California and Their Neighbors**. Healdsburg, California: Naturegraph Publishers, Inc., 1975, p. 25.

Tanning Hides
3. Wheat, Margaret M., p. 75.

    Levy, Richard. "Eastern Miwok" in **Handbook of North American Indians, California**. Volume 8. Edited by Robert F. Heizer. Washington, D.C.: Smithsonian Institution, 1978, p. 406.

    Smith, Charles R. "Tubatulabal" in **Handbook of North American Indians, California**. Volume 8. Edited by Robert F. Heizer. Washington, D.C.: Smithsonian Institution, 1978, p. 443.

    Spier, Robert F. G. "Foothill Yokuts" in **Handbook of North American Indians, California**. Volume 8. Edited by Robert F. Heizer. Washington, D.C.: Smithsonian Institution, 1978, p. 473.

    Levy, Richard. "Costanoan", in **Handbook of North American Indians, California**. Volume 8. Edited by Robert F. Heizer. Washington, D.C.: Smithsonian Institution, 1978, p. 493.

    Nelson, Byron. **Our Home Forever, A Hupa Tribal History**. Hoopa, California: Hupa Tribe, 1978, p.16.

    Knudtson, Peter M. **The Wintun Indians of California and Their Neighbors**. Happy Camp, California: Naturegraph Publishers, Inc., 1977, p. 31.

Footwear
4. Kroeber, A.L., pp. 76, 240, 292, 311, 323, 327, 405, 654, 721, 805, 807.

    Bright, William., p. 184.

    Silver, Shirley. "Shastan Peoples" in **Handbook of North American Indians, California**. Volume 8. Edited by Robert F. Heizer. Washington, D.C.: Smithsonian Institution, 1978, p. 217.

    Wilson, Norman L. and Towne, Arlean H., p. 391.

    Schulz, Paul E. **Indians of Lassen Volcanic National Park and Vicinity**. Mineral, California: Loomis Museum Association, Lassen Volcanic National Park, 1954, p. 109.

Thread and Cord
5. Kroeber, A.L., pp. 85-86, 333, 415, 651, 722, 827.

    Olmsted, D. L. and Stewart, Omer C. "Achumawi" in **Handbook of North American Indians, California**. Volume 8.

Edited by Robert F. Heizer. Washington, D.C.: Smithsonian Institution, 1978, p. 227.

Basket Caps

6.   Kroeber, A.L., pp. 76, 240, 807-808.

Wallace, William J., p. 167.

Schulz, Paul E., p. 107.

Miller, Bruce W. **Chumash, A Picture of Their World**. Los Osos, California: Sand River Press, 1988, p. 93.

Brusa, Betty War., p.25.

Ceremonial Regalia

7.   Latta, Frank F. **Handbook of Yokuts Indians**. Santa Cruz, California: Bear State Books, 1977, pp. 636-637.

Miller, Bruce W., pp. 92-93.

Kroeber, A.L., pp. 266-269, 508-509, 665.

Bates, Craig. "Feathered Regalia of Central California, Wealth and Power" in **The Occasional Papers of the Redding Museum**, Number 2. Redding, California: Redding Museum and Art Center, 1982.

Bright, William., p. 184.

Miller, Virginia P. "Yuki, Huchnom, and Coast Yuki" in **Handbook of North American Indians, California**. Volume 8. Edited by Robert F. Heizer. Washington, D.C.: Smithsonian Institution, 1978, p. 252.

Bean, Lowell John. "Cahuilla" in **Handbook of North American Indians, California**. Volume 8. Edited by Robert F. Heizer. Washington, D.C.: Smithsonian Institution, 1978, p. 579.

Bean, Lowell John and Vane, Sylvia Brakke. "Cults and Their Transformations" in **Handbook of North American Indians, California**. Volume 8. Edited by Robert F. Heizer. Washington, D.C.: Smithsonian Institution, 1978, p. 670.

Andreoli, Andrew. Director of Indian Teacher Education Personnel Program. Humboldt State University. 1993.

Tattooing

8.   Kroeber, A.L., pp. 77-78, 173, 293, 311, 406, 467, 519-521, 641, 721, 729, 808.

La Pena, Frank R., p. 336.

Levy, Richard. "Eastern Miwok", p. 407.

Body and Face Painting

9.   Kroeber, A.L., pp. 730-733.

Taylor, Edith S. and Wallace, William J. **Mohave Tattooing and Face-Painting**. Number 20. Southwest Museum Leaflets. Los Angeles, California: Southwest Museum, 1947.

Bright, William., p. 184.

Silver, Shirley. "Chimariko" in **Handbook of North American Indians, California**. Volume 8. Edited by Robert F. Heizer. Washington, D.C.: Smithsonian Institution, 1978, p. 207.

Silver, Shirley. "Shastan Peoples", p. 217.

Grant, Campbell. "Eastern Coastal Chumash" in **Handbook of North American Indians, California**. Volume 8. Edited by Robert F. Heizer. Washington, D.C.: Smithsonian Institution, 1978, p. 510.

Luomala, Katharine., p. 599.

McCall, Lynne and Perry, Rosalind, et al. **The Chumash People, Materials for Teachers and Students**. Santa Barbara, California: Santa Barbara Museum of Natural History, 1982, p. 124.

Andreoli, Andrew. Director of Indian Teacher Education Personnel Program. Humboldt State Univerisity, 1993.

Chapter 8

Plank Homes

1.   Kroeber, A.L. **Handbook of the Indians of California**. Bulletin 78, Smithsonian Institution, Bureau of American Ethnology. Washington, D.C.: Government Printing Office, 1925, pp. 78-82, 289-290, 731, 733,809.

Nelson, Byron. **Our Home Forever, A Hupa Tribal History**. Hoopa, California: Hupa Tribe, 1978, pp. 8-11.

Pilling, Arnold R. "Yurok" in Handbook of North American Indians, California. Volume 8. Edited by Robert F. Heizer. Washington, D.C.: Smithsonian Institution, 1978, p. 144.

Bark Homes

2.   Kroeber, A.L., pp. 111, 146-147, 213, 408, 809-810.

Elsasser, Albert B. "Mattole, Nongatl, Sinkyone, Lassik, and Wailaki" in **Handbook of North American Indians, California**. Volume 8. Edited by Robert F. Heizer. Washington, D.C.: Smithsonian Institution, 1978, p. 199.

Garth, T.R. "Atsugewi" in **Handbook of North American Indians, California**. Volume 8. Edited by Robert F. Heizer. Washington, D.C.: Smithsonian Institution, 1978, p. 237.

Bean, Lowell John and Theodoratus, Dorothea. "Western Pomo and Northeastern Pomo" in **Handbook of North American Indians, California**. Volume 8. Edited by Robert F. Heizer. Washington, D.C.: Smithsonian Institution, 1978, p. 292.

La Pena, Frank R. "Wintu" in **Handbook of North American Indians, California**. Volume 8. Edited by Robert F. Heizer. Washington, D.C.: Smithsonian Institution, 1978, p. 325.

Levy, Richard. "Eastern Miwok" in **Handbook of North American Indians, California**. Volume 8. Edited by Robert F. Heizer. Washington, D.C.: Smithsonian Institution, 1978, p. 408.

Spier, Robert F. G. "Monache" in **Handbook of North American Indians, California**. Volume 8. Edited by Robert F. Heizer. Washington, D.C.: Smithsonian Institution, 1978, p. 431.

Brush Homes

3. Kroeber, A.L., pp. 240-243, 557-558, 704, 809-810.

   Latta, Frank F. **Handbook of Yokuts Indians**. Santa Cruz, California: Bear State Books, 1977, pp. 345-372.

   Mc Call, Lynne and Perry, Rosalind, et al. **The Chumash People, Materials for Teachers and Students**. Santa Barbara, California:Santa Barbara Museum of Natural History, 1982,pp.32-34.

   Bright, William. "Karok" in **Handbook of North American Indians, California**. Volume 8. Edited by Robert F. Heizer. Washington, D.C.: Smithsonian Institution, 1978, p. 184.

   Sawyer, Jesse O. "Wappo" in **Handbook of North American Indians, California.** Volume 8. Edited by Robert F. Heizer. Washington, D.C.: Smithsonian Institution, 1978, p. 261.

   Bean, Lowell John and Theodoratus, Dorothea., p. 292.

   Levy, Richard., p. 398.

   Riddell, Francis A. "Maidu and Konkow" in **Handbook of North American Indians, California**. Volume 8. Edited by Robert F. Heizer. Washington, D.C.: Smithsonian Institution, 1978, p. 376.

Earth-Covered Brush Homes

4. Kroeber, A.L., pp. 175, 276, 654-655, 721.

   Latta, Frank F., pp. 345-372.

   La Pena, Frank R., p. 325.

   Johnson, Jerald Jay. "Yana" in **Handbook of North American Indians, California**. Volume 8. Edited by Robert F. Heizer. Washington, D.C.: Smithsonian Institution, 1978, p. 367.

   Levy, Richard., p. 408.

Sweathouses

5. Kroeber, A.L., pp. 80-82, 735, 810-811.

   Levy,Richard., p. 409.

   Spier, Robert F. G., p. 431.

   Smith, Charles R. "Tubatulabal" in **Handbook of North American Indians, California**. Volume 8. Edited by Robert F. Heizer. Washington, D.C.: Smithsonian Institution, 1978, p. 442.

Ceremonial or Dance Houses

6. Kroeber, A.L., pp. 175-176, 213, 241-242.

   Brown, Vinson and Andrews, Douglas. **The Pomo Indians of California and Their Neighbors**. Healdsburg, California: Naturegraph Publishers, 1969, pp. 30-31.

   Bean, Lowell and Lawton, Harry. **The Cahuilla Indians of Southern California**. Banning, California: Malki Museum Press, 1975.

   Miller, Virginia P. "Yuki, Huchnom, and Coast Yuki" in **Handbook of North American Indians, California**. Volume 8. Edited by Robert F. Heizer. Washington, D.C.: Smithsonian Institution, 1978, p. 255.

   Goldschmidt, Walter. "Nomlaki" in **Handbook of North American Indians, California**. Volume 8. Edited by Robert F. Heizer. Washington, D.C.: Smithsonian Institution, 1978, p. 343.

   Levy, Richard., p. 409.

   Bean, Lowell John. "Cahuilla" in **Handbook of North American Indians, California**. Volume 8. Edited by Robert F. Heizer. Washington, D.C.: Smithsonian Institution, 1978, pp. 577-578.

Chapter Nine

Beliefs and Customs

1. Brown, Vinson and Andrews, Douglas. **The Pomo Indians of California and Their Neighbors**. Healdsburg, California: Naturegraph Publishers, 1969, p.43.

   Bean, Lowell John and Vane, Sylvia Brakke. "California Religious Systems and Their Transformations" in **California Indian Shamanism**. Edited by Lowell John Bean. Menlo Park, California: Ballena Press, 1992, p.36.

   Bean, Lowell John. "California Indian Shamanism and Folk Curing" in **California Indian Shamanism**. Edited by Lowell John Bean. Menlo Park, California: Ballena Press, 1992, p. 57.

   Pilling, Arnold R. "Yurok" in **Handbook of North American Indians, California**. Volume 8. Edited by Robert F. Heizer. Washington, D.C.: Smithsonian Institution, 1978, p. 149.

   Wallace, William J. "Hupa, Chilula, and Whilkut" in **Handbook of North American Indians, California**. Volume 8. Edited by Robert Heizer. Washington, D.C.: Smithsonian Institution, 1978. pp.174-175.

   Kelly, Isabel. "Coast Miwok" in **Handbook of North American Indians,California**. Volume 8. Edited by Robert F. Heizer. Washington, D.C.: Smithsonian Institution, 1978, p. 423.

   Heizer, Robert F. "Natural Forces and Native World View" in **Handbook of North American Indians, California**. Volume 8. Edited by Robert F. Heizer. Washington, D.C.: Smithsonian Institution, 1978, p. 649.

Indian Leadership

2. Kroeber, A.L. **Handbook of the Indians of California**. Bulletin 78, Smithsonian Institution, Bureau of American Ethnology. Washington, D.C.: Government Printing Office, 1925, pp. 132-133, 163-164,177-178.

   Powers, Stephen. **Tribes of California**. Berkeley, California: University of California Press, 1976, pp. 45, 67, 157.

   Heizer, Robert F. and Elsasser, Albert B. **The Natural World of the California Indians**. Berkeley, California: University of California Press, 1980, pp. 34, 209.

Bean, Lowell John. "Social Organization" in **Handbook of North American Indians, California**. Volume 8. Edited by Robert F. Heizer. Washington, D.C.: Smithsonian Institution, 1978, p. 679.

3. Kroeber, A.L., pp. 308-309, 356, 399, 468-469.

Nelson, Byron., **Our Home Forever, A Hupa Tribal History**. Hoopa, California: Hupa Tribe, 1978, p. 26-28.

Silver, Shirley. "Shastan Peoples" in **Handbook of North American Indians, California**. Volume 8. Edited by Robert F. Heizer. Washington, D.C.: Smithsonian Institution, 1978, p. 218.

Levy Richard. "Eastern Miwok" in **Handbook of North American Indians, California**. Volume 8. Edited by Robert F. Heizer. Washington, D.C.: Smithsonian Institution, 1978, p. 410.

Bean, Lowell John. "Social Organization", p. 679.

4. Kroeber, A.L., pp. 49-50, 98.

Nelson, Byron. p. 26-28.

5. Kroeber, A.L., pp. 488, 496-498.

Latta, Frank F. **Handbook of Yokuts Indians**. Santa Cruz, California: Bear State Books, 1977, pp. 63-64, 283-284.

6. Kroeber, A.L., pp. 596, 609, 687-688.

Bean, Lowell John. "Social Organization", p. 678.

7. Kroeber, A.L., pp. 596, 745, 783, 799-802, 832-833.

8. Kroeber, A.L., p. 399.

Bean, Lowell John. "Social Organization", pp. 678-679.

Brown, Vinson and Andrews, Douglas. p. 37.

Nelson, Byron., pp. 28-29.

Miller, Bruce W. **Chumash, A Picture of Their World**. Los Osos, California: Sand River Press, 1988, p. 108.

Indian Doctors

9. Nelson, Byron., p. 72.

Kroeber, A.L., pp. 516, 851-855.

Powers, Stephen., p. 354.

Bean, Lowell John. "Social Organization", p. 679.

Elsasser, Albert B. "Wiyot" in **Handbook of North American Indians, California**. Volume 8. Edited by Robert F. Heizer. Washington, D.C.: Smithsonian Institution, 1978, pp. 159-160.

Callaghan, Catherine A. "Lake Miwok" in **Handbook of North American Indians, California**. Volume 8. Edited by Robert F. Heizer. Washington, D.C.: Smithsonian Institution, 1978, p. 269.

Bean, Lowell John. "Power and Its Applications in Native California" in **California Indian Shamanism**. Edited by Lowell John Bean. Menlo Park, California: Ballena Press, p. 31.

Bean, Lowell John. "California Indian Shamanism and Folk Curing", pp.55-58, 62.

Buckley, Thomas. "Yurok Doctors and the Concept of 'Shamanism' "in **California Indian Shamanism**. Edited by Lowell John Bean. Menlo Park, California: Ballena Press, p. 123.

Latta, Frank F., pp. 634-635.

Other Types of Doctors

10. Kroeber, A.L., pp. 518, 854.

Latta, Frank F., pp. 637-638.

11. Latta, Frank F., pp. 647-649, 651-652.

Kroeber, A.L., pp. 504-505, 517, 854.

Bean, Lowell John. "California Indian Shamanism and Folk Curing", pp. 58-59.

12. Kroeber, A.L., pp. 259, 516-517, 854-855.

Bean, Lowell John. "California Indian Shamanism and Folk Curing", p. 59.

Jeffrey, Cheryl. "Hunwe-lu'u-ish: The Cahuilla Bear Shaman" in **American Desert Magazine**. Desert Hot Springs, California: American Desert Magazine, Volume 1, Number 3, March/April, 1993, pp. 22-26.

Tobacco

13. Kroeber, A.L., pp. 88-89, 826-827.

Bean, Lowell John and Saubel, Katherine Siva. **Temalpakh, Cahuilla Indian Knowledge and Usage of Plants**. Banning, California: Malki Museum Press, 1972, pp.90-94.

Sweet, Muriel. **Common Edible and Useful Plants of the West**. Happy Camp, California: Naturegraph Publishers, Inc. 1976, p. 48.

Margolin, Malcolm. **The Ohlone Way, Indian Life in the San Francisco-Monterey Bay Area**. Berkeley, California: Heyday Books, 1978, p. 32.

Levy, Richard., p. 403.

Wallace, William J. "Southern Valley Yokuts" in **Handbook of North American Indians, California**. Volume 8. Edited by Robert F. Heizer. Washington, D.C.: Smithsonian Institution, 1978, p. 456.

Grant, Campbell. "Eastern Coastal Chumash" in **Handbook of North American Indians, California**. Volume 8. Edited b Robert F. Heizer. Washington, D.C.: Smithsonian Institution, 1978, p. 512.

Death

14. Kroeber, A.L., pp. 841-843.

Elsasser, Albert B. "Wiyot". p. 160.

Bright, William. "Karok" in **Handbook of North American Indians, California**. Volume 8. Edited by Robert F. Heizer. Washington, D.C.: Smithsonian Institution, 1978, p. 186.

Elsasser, Albert B. "Mattole, Nongatl, Sinkyone, Lassik, and Wailaki" in **Handbook of North American Indians, California**. Volume 8. Edited by Robert F. Heizer. Washington, D.C.: Smithsonian Institution, 1978, p. 197.

La Pena, Frank R. "Wintu" in **Handbook of North American Indians, California**. Volume 8. Edited by Robert F. Heizer. Washington, D.C.: Smithsonian Institution, 1978, p. 329.

15. Elsasser, Albert B. "Wiyot", p. 160.

Bright, William., p. 186.

Olmsted, D. L. and Stewart, Omer C. "Achumawi" in **Handbook of North American Indians, California**. Volume 8. Edited by Robert F. Heizer. Washington, D.C.: Smithsonian Institution, 1978, p. 232.

Garth, T. R. "Atsugewi" in **Handbook of North American Indians, California**. Volume 8. Edited by Robert F. Heizer. Washington, D.C.: Smithsonian Institution, 1978, p. 238.

La Pena, Frank R., p.329.

Andreoli, Andrew. Director of Indian Teacher Education Personnel Program. Humboldt State University, 1993.

16. Wallace, William J. "Hupa, Chilula, and Whilkut", p. 173.

La Pena, Frank R., p. 329.

17. Bright, William., p. 186.

Olmsted, D.L. and Stewart, Omer C., p. 232.

18. Callaghan, Catherine A., p. 267.

Bright, William., p. 186.

Ceremonies

19. Callaghan, Catherine A., p.269.

Mourning Ceremony

20. Latta, Frank F., pp. 674-680.

Kroeber, A.L., pp. 180, 253, 675, 859-861.

Riddell, Francis A. "Maidu and Konkow" in **Handbook of North American Indians, California**. Volume 8. Edited by Robert F. Heizer. Washington, D.C.: Smithsonian Institution, 1978, pp. 381-383.

Spier, Robert F.G. "Monache" in **Handbook of North American Indians, California**. Volume 8. Edited by Robert F. Heizer. Washington, D.C.: Smithsonian Institution, 1978, p. 433.

Spier, Robert F.G. "Foothill Yokuts" in **Handbook of North American Indians, California**. Volume 8. Edited by Robert F. Heizer. Washington, D.C.: Smithsonian Institution, 1978, p. 480.

Initiation Ceremony

21. Kroeber, A.L., pp. 684-685.

Heizer, Robert F. pp. 652-653.

Boys' Initiation Ceremony

22. Kroeber, A.L., pp. 503-504, 604, 640-641, 866.

Elsasser, Albert B. "Wiyot", p. 159.

Wallace, William J. "Hupa, Chilula, and Whilkut", p. 173.

Luomala, Katharine. "Tipai—Ipai" in **Handbook of North American Indians, California**. Volume 8. Edited by Robert F. Heizer. Washington, D.C.: Smithsonian Institution, 1978, p.603.

Bean, Lowell John and Vane, Sylvia Brakke. "Cults and Their Transformations" in **Handbook of North American Indians, California**. Volume 8. Edited by Robert F. Heizer. Washington, D.C.: Smithsonian Institution, 1978, pp. 668-673.

Girls' Initiation Ceremony

23. Kroeber, A.L., pp. 673-675, 861-865.

Wallace, William J. "Hupa, Chilula, and Whilkut", pp. 173,178.

Elsasser, Albert B. "Mattole, Nongatl, Sinkyone, Lassik, and Wailaki", p. 196.

Chapter Ten
Indian Music

1. Miller, Bruce W. **Chumash, a Picture of Their World**. Los Osos, California: Sand River Press, 1988, p. 113.

Myers, James E. "Cahto" in **Handbook of North American Indians, California**. Volume 8. Edited by Robert F. Heizer. Washington, D.C.: Smithsonian Institution, 1978, p. 246.

Wilson, Norman L. and Towne, Arlean H. "Nisenan" in **Handbook of North American Indians, California**. Volume 8. Edited by Robert F. Heizer. Washington, D.C.: Smithsonian Institution, 1978, p. 396.

Grant, Campbell. "Eastern Coastal Chumash" in **Handbook of North American Indians, California**. Volume 8. Edited by Robert F. Heizer. Washington, D.C.: Smithsonian Institution, 1978, p. 512.

Bean, Lowell John. "Cahuilla" in **Handbook of North American Indians, California**. Volume 8. Edited by Robert F. Heizer. Washington, D.C.: Smithsonian Institution, 1978, p. 580.

Wallace, William J. " Music and Musical Instruments" in **Handbook of North American Indians, California**. Volume 8. Edited by Robert F. Heizer. Washington, D.C.: Smithsonian Institution, 1978, p. 642.

Rattles

2. Heizer, Robert F. and Elsasser, Albert B. **The Natural World of the California Indians**. Berkeley, California: University of California Press, 1980, pp. 120-121.

   Miller, Bruce W., pp. 115-116.

   Kroeber, A.L. **Handbook of the Indians of California**. Bulletin 78, Smithsonian Institution, Bureau of American Ethnology. Washington, D.C.: Government Printing Office, 1925, pp. 762, 823.

   Almstedt, Ruth. **Diegueno Deer Toe Rattles**. Ethnic Technology Notes, Number 2. San Diego, California: San Diego Museum of Man, Balboa Park, 1968.

   Wallace, William J. "Music and Musical Instruments," pp. 644-645, 647.

Whistles and Flutes

3. Heizer, Robert F. and Elsasser, Albert B., p. 124.

   Miller, Bruce W., pp. 113-114.

   Kroeber, A.L., pp. 96, 419, 542, 705, 824.

   Elsasser, Albert B. " Mattole, Nongatl, Sinkyone, Lassik, and Wailaki" in **Handbook of North American Indians, California**. Volume 8. Edited by Robert F. Heizer. Washington, D.C.: Smithsonian Institution, 1978, p. 202.

   Wallace, William J. "Music and Musical Instruments", p. 645.

Drums

4. Heizer, Robert F. and Elsasser, Albert B., pp. 41,121.

   Kroeber, A.L., pp. 95-96, 189-190, 365, 765, 824.

   Wallace, William J. "Music and Musical Instruments", pp. 645-646.

Bull Roarer

5. Kroeber, A.L., pp. 266, 508-plate 44, 509, 666, 713, 824.

   Wallace, William J. "Music and Musical Instruments", pp. 646-647.

   Elsasser, Albert B., p. 202.

Indian Art

6. Van Tilburg, Jo Anne. "Of Art and Artists: The Rock Art of California" in **Ancient Images on Stone**. Compiled and Edited by Jo Anne Van Tilburg. Los Angeles, California: The Rock Art Archive and The Institute of Archaeology, University of California, 1983, p. 21.

Rock Art

7. Bean, Lowell John and Bourgeault, Lisa., p. 76.

   Claytor, Michael and Moller, Tommie. **California Indians, Rock Art**. Volume 2. Loomis, California: Michael Claytor and Tommie Moller, pp. 1-6, pamphlet—no date.

   Angel, Myron. **The Painted Rock of California, A Legend**. San Luis Obispo, California: Padre Productions, 1979.

   Grant, Campbell. **Rock Drawings of the Coso Range**. Ridgecrest, California: Maturango Museum, 1987, pp. 18-23, 25-28, 29-42.

   Clewlow, C. William Jr. "Prehistoric Rock Art" in **Handbook of North American Indians, California**. Volume 8. Edited by Robert F. Heizer. Washington, D.C: Smithsonian Institution, 1978, pp. 619-625.

Children's Games

8. Beard, Yolande S. **The Wappo, A Report**. Banning, California: Malki Museum Press, 1979, p. 60.

   Brown, Vinson and Andrews, Douglas. **The Pomo Indians of California and Their Neighbors**. Healdsburg, California: Naturegraph Publishers, 1969, p. 40.

   Elsasser, Albert B., p. 201.

   Myers, James E., p. 245.

   Goldschmidt, Walter. "Nomlaki" in **Handbook of North American Indians, California**. Volume 8. Edited by Robert F. Heizer. Washington, D.C.: Smithsonian Institution, 1978, p. 345.

   Wilson, Norman L. and Towne, Arlean H., p. 396.

   Smith, Charles. R. "Tubatulabal" in **Handbook of North American Indians, California**. Volume 8. Edited by Robert F. Heizer. Washington, D.C.: Smithsonian Institution, 1978, p. 441.

   James, Harry C. **The Cahuilla Indians**. Banning, California: Malki Museum Press, 1969, p. 64.

   Bean, John Lowell and Bourgeault, Lisa. **The Cahuilla**. New York City, New York: Chelsea House Publishers, 1989, p. 27.

Shinny

9. Kroeber, A.L., pp. 538-539, 847-848.

   Mc Lendon, Sally and Lowy, Michael J. "Eastern Pomo and Southeastern Pomo" in **Handbook of North American Indians, California**. Volume 8. Edited by Robert F. Heizer. Washington, D.C.: Smithsonian Institution, 1978, p. 318.

   Goldschmidt, Walter., p. 345.

   Smith, Charles R., p. 441.

   Wallace, William F. "Southern Valley Yokuts" in **Handbook of North American Indians, California**. Volume 8. Edited by Robert F. Heizer. Washington, D.C.: Smithsonian Institution, 1978, p. 456.

The Ring-and-Pin Game

10. Kroeber, A.L., pp. 846-847.

    Bean, Lowell John and Shipek, Florence. "Luiseno" in **Handbook of North American Indians, California**. Volume 8.

Edited by Robert F. Heizer. Washington, D.C.: Smithsonian Institution, 1978, p. 554.

La Pena, Frank R. "Wintu" in **Handbook of North American Indians, California**. Volume 8. Edited by Robert F. Heizer. Washington, D.C.: Smithsonian Institution, 1978, p. 333.

Silver, Shirley. "Shastan People" in **Handbook of North American Indians, California**. Volume 8. Edited by Robert F. Heizer. Washington, D.C.: Smithsonian Institution, 1978, p. 219.

Hudson, Travis and Timbrook, Jan. **Chumash Indian Games**. Santa Barbara, California: Santa Barbara Museum of Natural History, 1980, p. 4.

Elsasser, Albert B., p.202.

The Stick-and-Hoop Game

11. Kroeber, A.L., pp. 296, 539, 846.

    Smith, Charles R., p. 441.

    Wallace, William J. "Southern Valley Yokuts", p. 456.

    Hudson, Travis and Timbrook, Jan., p. 10.

    Miller, Bruce W., p. 116.

The Bark Spinning Game

12. Elsasser, Albert B., p. 201.

    Myers, James E., p. 245.

    La Pena, Frank R., p.333.

    Goldschmidt, Walter., p. 345.

Games for Adults and a Guessing Game

13. Kroeber, A.L., pp. 539-540, 848-850.

    Olmsted, D. L. and Stewart, Omer C. "Achumawi" in **Handbook of North American Indians, California**. Volume 8. Edited by Robert F. Heizer. Washington, D.C.: Smithsonian Institution, 1978, p. 234.

    La Pena, Frank R., p. 333.

A Staves Game

14. La Pena, Frank R., p.333.

    Kroeber, A.L., p. 741.

    Hudson, Travis and Timbrook, Jan., p. 14.

A Dice Game

15. Kroeber, A.L., pp. 540, 848.

    Hudson, Travis and Timbrook, Jan., p. 13.

    Goldschmidt, Walter., p. 345.

    Smith, Charles R., p. 441.

    Wallace, William J. "Southern Valley Yokuts", p. 456.

Chapter Eleven

1. Kroeber, Theodora. **Ishi, Last of His Tribe**. New York, New York: Bantam Books, Inc., 1964.

   Kroeber, Theodora. **Ishi in Two Worlds**. Berkeley, California: University of California Press, 1961.

   Meyer, Kathleen Allan. **Ishi, The Story of an American Indian**. Minneapolis, Minnesota: Dillon Press, Inc., 1980.

   Burrill, Richard. **Ishi: America's Stone Age Indian**. Sacramento, California: The Anthro Company, 1990.

   Johnson, Jerald Jay. "Yana" in **Handbook of North American Indians, California**. Volume 8. Edited by Robert F. Heizer. Washington, D. C.: Smithsonian Institution, 1978, pp. 361-369.

   Kroeber, A.L. **Handbook of the Indians of California**. Bulletin 78, Smithsonian Institution, Bureau of American Ethnology. Washington, D. C.: Government Printing Office, 1925, pp. 343-345.

Chapter Twelve

Spanish Invaders

1. Castillo, Edward D. "The Impact of Euro—American Exploration and Settlement" in **Handbook of North American Indians, California**. Volume 8. Edited by Robert F. Heizer. Washington, D.C.: Smithsonian Institution, 1978, p. 99.

2. Heizer, Robert F. and Elsasser, Albert B. **The Natural World of the California Indians**. Berkeley, California: University of California Press, 1980, p. 226.

3. Heizer, Robert F. and Elsasser, Albert B., p. 227.

   Rawls, James J. Indians of California, **The Changing Image**. Norman, Oklahoma: University of Oklahoma Press, 1984, pp. 34, 37-38.

   Caughey, John and Laree. **California Heritage, An Anthology of History and Literature**. Los Angeles: The Ward RitchiePress, 1966, pp. 77-82.

Spain Loses California to Mexico

4. Castillo, Edward D., pp. 102-103.

5. Arbuckle, Clyde. **Santa Clara County Ranchos**. San Jose, California: The Rosicrucian Press, Ltd., 1968, pp. 25,36.

6. Heizer, Robert F. and Elsasser, Albert B., pp. 226,229.

7. Castillo, Edward D., p. 106.

The Indians and The Gold Rush

8. Heizer, Robert F. and Elsasser, Albert B., p. 228.

9. Rawls, James J., pp. 116,122.

10. Rawls, James J., p. 115.

11. Rawls, James J., pp. 117, 122.

12. Rawls, James J., p. 132.

    Forbes, Jack D. **Native Americans of California and Nevada**. Healdsburg, California; Naturegraph Publishers, 1969, p. 54.

13. Forbes, Jack D., p. 52-56.

California Becomes a State

14. Rawls, James J. p. 83.

15. Heizer, Robert F. and Elsasser, Albert B., p. 233.

16. Ainslie, Joan, et al., American Indian Education Office. **The American Indian: Yesterday, Today and Tomorrow, A Handbook for Educators**. Sacramento, California: California Department of Education, 1991, pp. 13,73.

17. Ainslie, Joan, et al., p. 73.

18. Ainslie, Joan, et al., p. 73.

19. Castillo, Edward D., p. 115.

20. Patterson, Victoria, et al. **The Singing Feather, Tribal Remembrances from Round Valley**. Ukiah, California: Mendocino County Library, 1990, p. 7.

The Bureau of Indian Affairs

21. Ainslie, Joan, et al., pp. 11-13, 70-71. Bureau of Indian Affairs. California Area Office, Federal Office Building, Sacramento, California, as per telephone conversation, October, 1993.

    ————————————.**American Indians Today, Answers to Your Questions**, 1991. Washington, D. C.: United States Department of the Interior, Bureau of Indian Affairs, 1991, booklet.

    Statement of Ada E. Deer before the Senate Committee on Indian Affairs, July 15, 1993.

California Indian Reservations and Rancherias

22. Ainslie, Joan, et al., pp. 6-7, 73-74, 76.

    ————————————.**American Indians Today, Answers to Your Questions,** 1991. Washington, D.C.: United States Department of the Interior, Bureau of Indian Affairs, 1991, booklet.

Indian Population

23. United States Census Bureau, Van Nuys, California, as per telephone conversation, October, 1993.

    Bureau of Indian Affairs. California Area Office, Federal Office Building, Sacramento, California, as per telephone conversation, October, 1993.

    ————————————. **American Indians Today, Answers to Your Questions**, 1991. Washington, D.C.: United States Department of the Interior, Bureau of Indian Affairs, 1991, booklet.

Indian Education

24. Ainslie, Joan, et al., pp. 13, 21-24, 76-79.

    Babby, Fayetta. Bureau of Indian Affairs, Area Education Program Administrator, Sacramento, California, as per telephone conversation, October, 1993.

    ————————————. **American Indians Today, Answers to Your Questions**, 1991. Washington, D.C.: United States Department of the Interior, Bureau of Indian Affairs, 1991, booklet.

California Indians Today

25. Hurtado, Albert L. **Indian Survival on the California Frontier**. New Haven, Connecticut: Yale University Press, 1988, p. 212.

INDEX